Congregations in Transition

Congregations in Transition

A Guide for Analyzing, Assessing, and Adapting in Changing Communities

Carl S. Dudley and Nancy T. Ammerman

FOREWORD BY LOREN B. MEAD

JOSSEY-BASS
A Wiley Company
www.josseybass.com

Published by Jossey-Bass
A Wiley Imprint
989 Market Street, San Francisco, CA 94103-1741   www.josseybass.com

Jossey-Bass books and products are available through most bookstores. To contact Jossey-Bass directly call our Customer Care Department within the U.S. at 800-956-7739, outside the U.S. at 317-572-3986, or fax 317-572-4002.

Jossey-Bass also publishes its books in a variety of electronic formats. Some content that appears in print may not be available in electronic books.

Credits are on p. 189.

Library of Congress Cataloging-in-Publication Data

Dudley, Carl S., date.
  Congregations in transition: a guide for analyzing, assessing, and adapting in changing communities / Carl S. Dudley and Nancy T. Ammerman.
    p. cm.
  Includes bibliographical references and index.
  ISBN 0-7879-5422-5 (alk. paper)
  1. Parishes. 2. Pastoral theology. I. Ammerman, Nancy Tatom, date. II. Title.
BV700 .D83 2002
250—dc21   2001006048

Printed in the United States of America
FIRST EDITION
PB Printing   10 9 8 7 6 5

CONTENTS

FIGURES, TABLES, AND WORKING NOTES

FIGURES

TABLE

WORKING NOTES

FOR SARAH POLSTER

FOREWORD

D on't mess with this book.

This book is not about patching something up. It is a radical book. It says the problem is not in the things you can "adjust" and "fix"; the problem goes to the roots.

So if you are interested in getting through the next year with as little discomfort as possible, putting on a parish program that will look good in the annual report at the time of the next congregational meeting, this book is not for you.

If, on the other hand, you know that your congregation has some beginnings—some people who see that the old game isn't working any-more, some people who feel God calling them to deeper ministry, some people who want to make a difference in the world around your congre-gation, some people who aren't scared to try something new and to fight to make something happen, or if that's where you might be if you could get a few others to talk about it—well, this just might be the place to start.

In *Congregations in Transition: A Guide for Analyzing, Assessing, and Adapting in Changing Communities,* Carl Dudley and Nancy Ammerman offer a set of practical resources for congregational leaders—resources for mapping out who and where the congregation is, resources for posing the ultimate challenge of what the congregation is prepared to face, resources for analyzing and mobilizing your energy, and resources for looking beyond today's church and acting for the church of tomorrow. They believe congregations can sustain and empower human life. They believe congregations can make a difference. They have put together a book for those who are serious about what congregations can be and can do.

This is not a complicated book, and neither are the tools it offers. I believe it can genuinely help you move from where you are to where you are called to be.

But first you need to decide if you are willing to move from where you are. The authors are clear about the costs and difficulties—but the most important costs and difficulties need to be faced at the beginning. Is your congregation willing to choose to live? Even if it requires facing change or even death? If you are, I introduce you to Carl Dudley and Nancy Ammerman. They are trustworthy companions on your journey. Their book can be a true guide to your pilgrimage.

Every spring, from my office window, I watch a nest of mockingbirds that seem to return to the same bush every year. I cannot quite see the eggs in the nest, but after a few weeks, I do see the small beaks poking up to be fed by the parents. The excitement builds when the babies start bumbling around on the edge of the nest, flapping their growing wings. I am always aware of the drama as the chicks hang on to the edges of the nest somewhat desperately, trying to fly. I know, although I guess they don't, what has got to happen if they are to have life. First, they have to let go of their old life and let go of their nest; next, they have to try out the wings they've never fully tested, trusting that somehow they can fly; then they have to fly away. Finally, they have to leave home. Some never make it. But every spring, I have new mockingbirds out there, and some even answer when I whistle.

If your congregation is really ready to try its wings, if it has within it life ready to commit itself to the air and to fly, this book is for you.

If not, don't mess with this book.

Washington, D.C.   Loren B. Mead
December 2001   Founding President of the Alban Institute

ACKNOWLEDGMENTS

This book could not have been written in an ivory tower. Because everything about it is so grounded in the practices of congregational life, we owe a large debt of gratitude to all the congregations whose experiences are reflected here—to the many places where Carl has advised and consulted and to the congregations Nancy studied as part of the Congregations in Changing Communities Project.

In addition, more than twenty brave congregations from the Presbytery of San Francisco agreed to invest six months or more in 1999 to test the exercises we were working on and to share their experiences at a national gathering on urban ministry. As a result, not all of the initial exercises made it into the book, and the ones that did are much improved because of the suggestions these congregations made. We are enormously grateful to them for their courage and candor, and to Trey Hammond and the National Planning Committee of Urban Ministry Office, Presbyterian Church (USA), which facilitated the Conference on Urban Ministry.

We have also benefited from the careful and constructive criticisms of our colleagues at Hartford Seminary and on the Congregational

Studies Team, as well as from detailed comments made by anonymous reviewers. They have challenged us to make sure that the book has theoretical and theological integrity as well as practical sensibility.

Finally, this book simply would not have come into being but for the wisdom, passion, and vision of Sarah Polster. She was our friend before she was our editor, but she brought both roles to bear on the challenge of helping us create a book neither of us could fully envision at the beginning. Her death leaves us with a loss deeper than we can express. Sarah believed passionately that congregations were worth investing with the best possible leadership and resources. Our hope is that this book is a fitting contribution to her legacy.

Congregations in Transition

CHAPTER ONE

INTRODUCTION
Invitation to a Journey

Congregations have never been more important. In a mobile and fragmented world they are a spiritual home, a gathering place where caring, trusting relationships are built and nurtured. In a world where outsiders' voices are often kept silent, congregations invite those voices to speak. In a world of great need, congregations provide support and comfort, food and shelter, training and advocacy. In a world that seeks moral and spiritual guidance but has no clear tradition to guide it, congregations preserve and renew traditions, calling their members and communities to accountability and vision. Although doomsayers of a generation ago may have thought congregations were islands of complacency or dinosaurs on their way to extinction, it is clear that the obituaries were premature.

It is because we care about congregations that we have written this book. Because we are convinced that congregations are critical to the well-being of individual faithful people and to the well-being of our communities, we want congregations to thrive.

We also recognize that thriving is not easy. Sustaining a community of faith in today's world is as challenging as it is critical. Through circumstances that may seem as much mysterious as miraculous, many congregations find themselves in what seems to be a strange land. The familiar terrain they remember from not long ago seems to have disappeared, and the pathways between church and community seem to lead only to detours and road construction.

This book is primarily designed with urban and suburban churches in mind, and the reality of urban life has always been that neighborhoods change over time. In addition, the reality of the twenty-first century is that individual lives are a constant litany of change. Even when we stay in one place, we make different choices as our lives evolve. The neat match of neighborhood, members, and programs that existed (at least in hallowed memory) a few years ago is gone today—and what exists today will be gone as well in a few more years.

In today's world, congregations change—sometimes by choice, sometimes by default. Engaging the exercises in this book is testimony to your congregation's commitment to make those changes by choice.

WHO NEEDS TO CHANGE?

Because life never stops presenting us with surprises, no congregation is immune from change. Sometimes the source of that change is internal. Youth grow up and move away, and a once-thriving youth group withers while their parents move from being empty-nesters to old age. In other congregations, immigrants settle in and learn the language, and a once-vital foreign-language ministry is no longer needed. The natural rhythms of life can shift the focus from nursery rooms to hearing aids.

Beyond the natural cycles of change lies a culture that expects each of us to create a life and a community for ourselves. People leave home to attend school, where perhaps they meet and marry someone whose family honors different traditions from their own. They move in order to pursue a new job or buy a new house, and in the process leave an old congregation behind. They encounter a crisis and seek new spiritual guidance, perhaps from unexpected sources. Congregations simply cannot count on stable communities, stable people, or denominational loyalties to keep their flocks in place. The United States has always had a voluntary religious system, but today it seems more voluntary than ever.

Sometimes the source of change is right outside the congregation's four walls. What was once a church-friendly neighborhood may have been rezoned as industrial and commercial space. A busy thoroughfare may be rerouted away from a congregation's doorstep, or parking laws may make commuting impossible. Housing that suited young middle-class families fifty years ago may be occupied by multiple immigrant families today. Grand turn-of-the-century houses may have fallen into disrepair or been "regentrified." Cities constantly reuse and rearrange their space, shuffling populations and buildings from one place to another over the years and challenging even the most adept congregation to maintain itself.

Some of the greatest stress is found today in the neighborhoods just past a city's center. From the Civil War through World War II, "in-town" neighborhoods housed the workers and managers of a growing urban economy and were connected to the city's economic and political landmarks by trolley and subway lines. Within these neighborhoods, Protestant, Catholic, and Jewish places of worship multiplied, with a major church-building boom in the 1920s. These distinctive religious buildings, each reflecting its own tradition, served the religious needs of the families who occupied the modest bungalows and apartments that surrounded them. When those families began to move to the suburbs in the 1950s, some of them looked for new places of worship, some took their congregations with them, and others returned each week to places of long-held family memories. The commitment to retain old congregational ties became increasingly difficult to keep, however, as the number of children increased and the children themselves grew older. In the 1960s and 1970s, as urban communities declined in resources and changed in racial or ethnic composition, fewer families were willing to come back to attend church in neighborhoods they often saw as unfriendly or fearsome. Under these conditions, many older churches sold their buildings to new congregations and moved out.

But others stayed behind. Historically black churches often became stronger as they flowered into multilayered, faith-based neighborhood cultural centers. Mainline (white) Protestant denominations (such as Episcopal and Methodist) were often committed to retaining historic congregations in urban communities and urged these congregations to integrate new urban neighbors and adapt their ministries to changing conditions. A few did so in stunning fashion, becoming activist leaders in the community. After nearly fifty years, many others, however, are still struggling. Faced with critically depleted resources, many churches now seek a place in urban neighborhoods and regions that have been transformed several times over. They may never again be neighborhood churches, nor will they regain the families that left long ago. Reimagining their futures is especially challenging for these venerable old congregations.

Although these inner-fringe urban neighborhoods are among the most dramatically changed communities, suburbs present their own challenges. As new suburbs were built in the 1950s and 1960s, new congregations were built along with them. Fueled by the baby boom, church attendance reached new highs, and family-centered congregations grew alongside the family-centered schools and parks and neighborhoods.[1] These 1950s churches remain today the most organizationally healthy congregations, with higher average attendance and fatter yearly budgets than congregations founded either earlier or later. In part this is because the cultural ties linking suburban home ownership with child rearing and religious attendance were strong when these churches were founded and remain so now. While overall membership in mainline Protestant groups has declined, for instance, their "market share" of families with young children has remained constant. The challenge for these suburban congregations, however, is that the number of families with young children has declined from about half of U.S. households in the 1950s to less than a quarter today.[2] Although families are still looking for churches to which to take their children, there are not enough such families to support all the congregations that once thrived in this population niche. At least some of these suburban congregations will be looking for new programs and new members in the years ahead.

As urban areas have sprawled, congregations on the fringes face challenges of their own. In the 1980s and 1990s, developers turned their sights ever further outward, placing businesses along urban perimeter highways and housing in what used to be rural pastures. People in remote small towns suddenly found themselves part of an urban region—the "exurbs." Neither they nor their suburban neighbors necessarily thought they would ever have to go into the city's center, but they were clearly part of the city. As office parks and shopping malls have proliferated on the edge of the city, these communities have become part of the decentralized urban region, transforming it from a hub-and-spokes pattern into a pepperoni pizza pattern. In these newly exurban communities, country churches have found themselves swamped by newcomers and competing with "megachurches."[3]

Megachurches are, of course, regional churches. They are likely to draw their members from every corner of the city. But they are not the only congregations that draw members from a wide area. Many congregations used to be closely tied to a particular geographical place—identified with a neighborhood, subdivision, or town. When a person joined Pleasantville Methodist, for example, she identified herself both with a religious tradition and with a place. Increasingly, however, religious choices are more complicated. Although a person may live in Pleasantville, he may shop at the regional mall, belong to the downtown Rotary, work at an exurban industrial park or office complex, and enroll his children in a charter school for the arts. The fact that a person has chosen the Episcopal church across town has less to do with where that person lives than with the particular programs, ministries, and people found in that church. Congregations increasingly occupy a niche that is identified more by programming and membership than by denomination or location. People still want to belong, but their sense of belonging is more complicated than the towns and families that used to anchor them.

As a result, not many congregations are primarily related to an immediate geographical community. Many are located in "religious districts," analogous to shopping districts, where the presence of diverse congregations in close proximity to one another encourages "customers" to "shop" in the neighborhood. Similarly, one can find busy intersections or highway interchanges with large congregations on every corner. Far from competing for neighborhood residents, each church draws a distinct membership from as large a region as it can afford parking space to accommodate.

Thus, people in U.S. cities who seek out places in which they can worship have a dizzying variety from which to choose. The congregations that fill those cities are as varied as the cultures and lifestyles of the population. Although there may be several dozen Methodist churches, for instance, no two are exactly alike; each expresses different ways that people identify themselves, their values, and their culture. Congregations are places to call home, but the home they create is less and less likely to be adjacent to where their members actually live.

Who has to change? In many ways, everyone does. But urban regions pose constant challenges. In-town neighborhoods have been in continuous flux for at least fifty years. Suburbs built for the baby boom generation are now aging, as are the boomers themselves. Exurbs have transformed distant small towns, and mobile populations are seeking congregations, with little regard for proximity and neighborhood. Because human beings seem always to be altering their environment, the religious communities into which they gather will inevitably change as well.

WHAT DOES CHANGE LOOK LIKE?

In 1992, the Congregations in Changing Communities Project, a research effort funded by the Lilly Endowment and based at Emory University, sent a team of researchers to survey nine urban communities that were especially stressed by changes both good and bad. Some were devastated by economic downturns, others were thriving and growing because of economic good times. Some were home to waves of new immigrants, others were becoming identified as gay and lesbian enclaves. What we learned about how congregations change informs the ideas and exercises in this workbook. By drawing on the experiences of the congregations we studied, your own congregation can perhaps glimpse some new possibilities.[4]

We discovered several common patterns of congregational response to change:

- Many congregations simply attempt to hold their own, doing what they have always done, with a slowly dwindling membership. Some of these eventually close their doors or merge with another congregation.

- Some congregations move. They look at the possibilities for ministry in their current location and opt for friendlier territory. They assess the needs and what they have to offer and conclude that their gifts could be best used elsewhere.

- A few congregations stare death in the face and determine they will not go to the grave. They experience resurrection, often under the leadership of a pastor who helps them start all over again by developing new ministries and new styles of worship.

- A few farsighted and courageous congregations undertake the hard work of rerooting themselves, planning for new ministries and integrating newcomers into their midst even before the situation becomes critical.

- Some congregations seek their new identity in a set of ministries less tied to a particular place and more tied to the gifts, connections, and passions of their members. They find a niche within the large array of congregations and ministries available in a metropolitan region.

- More common than any other response to change is the founding of new congregations. We discovered that 21 percent of the congregations in the neighborhoods we studied in the early 1990s had been founded since 1980. A larger survey five years later, covering five representative large urban regions, found that 14 percent of the congregations had been founded since 1985.[5]

- Some congregations merge. By choosing to join forces with another existing congregation, these churches experience changes that span all the other alternatives. There are elements of both birth and death in merging. Congregations that do it successfully have to create a new congregational culture in ways that are not unlike the tasks facing congregations that reroot or create a new niche for themselves. Many merged congregations also move. While merging is a distinct pattern of change, its many variations create challenges characteristic of nearly all the other patterns combined and compounded.

Which path lies ahead for your church? No single path is right for every congregation. This workbook is an invitation to explore all the options, but to do so after thorough immersion in the world in which your congregation ministers, along with an equally thorough look at the history, gifts, and passions your congregation brings to that world.

HOW DOES CHANGE HAPPEN?

Although there are many different paths a congregation can follow, we found some very clear differences between congregations that embrace change and those that resist or ignore it. It is those differences that inform the exercises contained in this book. The exercises are designed to invite your congregation into the habits and practices that characterize those that make successful transitions. This book does not outline a program. It simply offers opportunities to experiment with new ways of being together as a congregation, ways that make change more possible.

One of the first things we discovered about adapting congregations was that they simply notice what is going on around them. Declining congregations often barely realize that the world has changed. So first we offer a series of exercises designed to heighten your *curiosity.* We invite you and your congregation to engage your curiosity about the world by investigating what is happening in your own neighborhood and in the larger community where the congregation's members live.

Adapting congregations are also curious about themselves and able to make critical judgments about their own capacities. They are able to build on foundations and resources they already have. They know their own history and are able to find stories from the past that are useable for the future. So we also invite you and your congregation to engage in exercises that will allow you to practice *honest self-assessment.* Taking a good, thorough look at oneself requires courage, but it also invites laughter and grace.

Another difference between adapters and resisters is a simple willingness to try something new. But trying new things is always scary, and congregations that succeed cultivate a habit of *playful experimentation.* Rather than stake everything on a given effort, they take modest risks and cut their losses when an effort fails. We invite you and your congregation to experiment with new ways of doing what you do, as well as to imagine new ministries and new outreach. We also offer exercises that will allow you to practice a spirit of playfulness so you can laugh at your failures as well as celebrate your successes.

Equally striking in congregations that welcome change is their *entrepreneurship.* Imagining new ministries requires imagining new resources—not only new money, but also new partners and new ways to use existing resources. We invite you to think "outside the box" about who might help you do what you want to do, and where treasures are hidden in your own midst.

Once a congregation has turned a corner and begun the process of change, the work is not over. Change may begin with noticing, assessing, experimenting, and creating new resources, but it is not complete until it has been fully incorporated into the culture of the congregation. Congregations that really make that transition know that changing the culture is more than a matter of rational planning and logical arguments.

It also requires engaging the imagination and the heart, often through *drama and symbols.* Sometimes actions speak louder than words and stories communicate better than lectures. We therefore offer suggestions for dramatic ways to embody your struggle and visualize signs of your future.

Congregational change fundamentally involves welcoming and incorporating new people. As new people arrive, they need to be both welcomed and invited to the table of food, tables of ritual, and tables of decision making. Real change happens when the disciplines of *hospitality* extend far beyond the front door, establishing ways to move newcomers into the shared experiences of the congregation. We suggest concrete ways in which your congregation can form new habits of hospitality.

Perhaps no finding from our study is more commonsensical—and more disturbing—than the discovery that congregations that change are also congregations where there is conflict. People who care about their congregation will inevitably disagree about how to move forward, so adaptive congregations have found ways of *embracing conflict.* Discovering that it is possible to disagree but still move forward is one of the critical differences between peaceful-but-stagnant congregations and those that are willing to disturb the status quo.

These seven habits—curiosity, honest self-assessment, playful experimentation, entrepreneurship, using drama and symbols, practicing hospitality, and embracing conflict—are the practices that distinguish congregations that undertake the hard work of change. But this work is not simply an exercise in good organizational management. At their heart, what all these habits require is *spiritual discernment.* You will need to call on the spiritual resources of a congregation. These resources of scripture and prayer will help you see the world with curious eyes, look honestly at yourselves, experiment in a spirit of grace, imagine new resources, create the stories and rituals that point beyond today, welcome the stranger, and love one another in the midst of conflict.

Because we believe this is fundamentally a spiritual process, we have used a story from the Hebrew Scriptures to frame our work. The story of the Exodus has always been a powerful way for God's people to think about being called to change. The people of Israel had been in Egypt for 430 years. They had settled in, accumulating cattle and children and a way of life. Even if it did involve slavery, it was what they knew. Leaving Egypt was not easy. It meant learning their way around in a wilderness and acquiring new skills. It meant calling on all the wisdom and stamina they could muster. But it also meant envisioning a new way of life in a land they could not yet see.

To respond adaptively and creatively to change is an enormous challenge, but one we are convinced can be successfully undertaken. To do so requires more than mere social analysis. It involves spiritual commitment. When faced with change, congregations have options. This workbook offers congregational leaders basic tools for learning new habits. As members become informed, they are challenged to discover appropriate ministries and to respond with increased commitment. In a world that is constantly changing, all congregations have the freedom in faith to choose directions for ministry.

THE JOURNEY AHEAD

This book is designed to help congregations that know they need to change. We believe that change has more to do with the imagination of the church's members than with its programs, so the strategies we present are designed to incorporate both feelings and facts. Each chapter will take you and your congregation another step along the way, and in each case you will call on your sense of vision, artistry, and imagination as much as on your ability to calculate and make plans. Each of these steps requires different analytical tools and fresh spiritual commitments. We reflect these differences in the concepts, technology, and activities we offer in each chapter.

Chapter Two begins with a variety of *mapping exercises* designed to activate your curiosity about the community in which you now work, locating yourselves in the context of change. The first exercise invites you to define the community's boundaries, and that may be the hardest conversation of all. But once you have wrestled with just who you are and where you fit in the community, you can add to your map a rich picture of the people and institutions that share the church's social and geographical space. We invite you to interview leaders and ordinary residents, to gather history and current statistics, and to explore the church's territory with new eyes. You will look for who is there and how they live, as well as for the organizations and resources that may be potential partners as you find the congregation's new place in this world.

Chapter Three guides you to develop several *timelines* to help you see the congregation's current situation within the flow of events from past to future. You will begin by collectively constructing a visual representation of your church's history. You will then add considerable depth and detail as you look at how your space and its use have changed over time; how the dynamics of leadership and decision making have provided energy and direction; how the pool of available people, money, and commitment has ebbed and flowed; and even how your ways of gathering to worship and sing have evolved over the years. These exercises will help you do the sort of honest self-assessment that can reveal the deepest values that have sustained your congregation over time, as well as the stories and resources you have available for the church's future. Looking at the congregation's history should make clear that change is not such a new thing after all. When you gather at the end of this process to weave all the historical details into your basic congregational timeline, it should be a celebration of where you have been and bring you to the threshold of your next chapter.

Chapter Four begins with a reminder that this is a journey into the wilderness. Having immersed yourselves in the world in which you seek to minister and having assessed the historical resources you have for the journey, this is the time to leave the familiar behind and seek the congregation's future. We invite you to use *role-playing* to help you imagine how to move forward. You will imaginatively take the perspectives of the strangers who might become your neighbors and the neighbors who might become your partners. You will dare to imagine your own congregation as it might look if you chose different paths of change. More than a list of pros and cons, these exercises will provide deeply felt experiences out of which we will invite you to name the particular vision that is calling your congregation forward.

Chapter Five suggests that even when you have followed a pillar of fire all the way to the promised land, there is still the matter of settling in. Having clarified a vision for ministry, what remains is the hard work of making that vision an ongoing part of the everyday culture of your congregation. This will require attention to some basic *congregational habits and practices* to help members assimilate new cultural patterns and perspectives. Part of the new culture will indeed be new programs and ministries, and we will invite you into an exercise that will help you cultivate your entrepreneurship and prepare to be playful experimenters. As new people join you on this journey, you will need to call on the practices of hospitality that are especially apparent in "breaking bread"—one of the areas of church life in which new habits can be cultivated. We will also suggest ways to cultivate new habits of using and sharing space, new habits that will allow your congregation to embrace the conflicts that will inevitably come, and new habits that will build up a store of symbols and stories for the future.

The exercises in which you will engage, then, are the first steps on a journey. Community change is inevitable, but congregations can choose how they will respond. This process of exploration is intended to help you prepare for the decisions—organizational and spiritual—and the hard work of becoming the congregation you are called to be. Doing that work depends on beginning by clearly recognizing where you are, who you have become, and what the community is to which you must minister. You will need to make strong yet flexible commitments to discover and absorb essential changes in ways that will strengthen your congregation in the process.

GETTING ORGANIZED

We encourage congregations using this workbook to organize a committee or task group that has the primary responsibility of gathering information, sharing it with the congregation, and organizing the results into an action plan. But every church must follow its own style of organizing. It is important for the work of any group to be authorized in whatever way is appropriate in your tradition. Many people will ultimately be involved in the work, but a core, authorized group is essential for guiding the process.

Congregations in changing communities often feel they have no resources—people, buildings, or spiritual reserves—to indulge in idle activities. They are uninterested in study exercises for their own sake. That is why each of the exercises we propose is aimed at making it possible for congregations to move forward in creative new ways. Congregations that are faced with new conditions often have a hard time achieving a clear vision of their next steps and therefore tend to repeat old, failing patterns, each time with greater intensity. In fact, ironically, declining churches often have higher levels of commitment than other churches, but commitment to unproductive activities. These exercises are an opportunity to break that cycle.

Each of the activities we propose should help the congregation become more in touch with its community and with itself. Although we propose a particular sequence, congregations are invited to approach the exercises with a maximum of flexibility and creativity. You can skip those that explore topics about which you already have sufficient information, add new exercises of your own design, and do the exercises in the order that best fits your schedule. But we hope you will not skip an exercise because it seems too hard or at first looks irrelevant. It is often not until you take the risk of trying something new that you begin to see why it is important. Enjoy the diversity of these steps, because taken together they reflect the complexity of the decisions facing churches in changing communities.

As you plan your work, decide how much time you want to allow for this process. You might work on Chapters Two and Three during the fall, turning to Chapter Four and subsequent planning in the spring. The tasks of Chapter Five will then go on for as long as it takes to assimilate all the changes you hope to see in your congregation. Working with twenty congregations in the San Francisco area, we found that about half were able to keep up with the exercises and complete the equivalent of Chapters Two to Four in six months (from March through September), with strong congregational interest and participation even through the summer. There is no best schedule; the process can be undertaken at any time your leadership is ready to make the commitment. Not every exercise is equally important for each congregation, and some congregations can move more quickly, especially if they already have available some of the resources for developing community maps (Chapter Two) and congregational timelines (Chapter Three). Although the steps can be completed relatively rapidly, that may come at the cost of less congregational awareness of and support for the essential process of change.

Whatever schedule your congregation adopts, the committee should use every means available to encourage maximum participation from others in and beyond the congregation. Some of the most helpful resources may come from the congregation's members and their networks throughout the community; others may be found in the newest arrivals who have not yet been fully assimilated into the congregation. Use all of these resources. Within both the congregation and the larger community, make sure that your work is shared as broadly as possible. Invite others to join in the various exercises, such as designing maps, recalling history, and walking the neighborhood. The most powerful congregational and community studies are not the work of an exclusive (and exhausted) committee, but the shared activity of wide segments of the congregation, and interested people from the larger community as well.

COMPANIONS FOR THE JOURNEY

This is a journey your congregation should not take alone. Such an adventure calls for conversation partners to give perspective and support at critical moments. You may be able to solicit interested neighboring congregations to join yours in exploring the community's changing conditions and new options, perhaps working through an ecumenical or even interfaith coalition. The church's regional denominational staff may also organize a joint effort of several congregations to work together to study themselves and their changing communities.

The committee may also find companionship for the journey in the stories of other congregations. Throughout this book we offer stories from the congregations we have studied. You may want to explore these stories in more detail in Dudley's *Basic Steps Toward Community Ministries* or Ammerman's *Congregation and Community*.[6] In addition, the list of suggestions for further reading at the end of each chapter includes accounts of the challenges faced by other congregations and insightful guides for many of the issues you may confront. A visit to a local library or bookstore can remind you that you are not the first people to traverse these roads.

The Internet is another resource you may find especially helpful. Whether you use it to "chat" with others who share your concerns or to access information, the World Wide Web is an excellent tool for enlarging your congregational imagination. Denominations, church consultants, and publishers, as well as community organizations and government offices, maintain sites with a wealth of useful information and links to resources you might not otherwise have thought to check.[7]

A final resource you may find helpful is the book *Studying Congregations: A New Handbook*.[8] While we have tried to provide you with all the instruction you will need to do the exercises in this book, *Studying Congregations* provides a much more in-depth exploration of ways to understand congregational life and methods for undertaking congregational study. For those who would like to use this additional resource, we indicate in the chapter notes in this book where in that book to look for more help.

DOING THE WORK

Each of the exercises begins with a brief overview and rationale for what you are about to undertake, followed by specific instructions about what to do. (In many cases, we have also provided a page for your "working notes" to help you in planning and completing the exercise.) Such instructions can, of course, never cover all the contingencies. Part of your task as a committee is to arrive at your own plan of action. Many of the exercises will require you to divide up assignments and report back at a later meeting. Others will invite you to do something together as a group. Some will work best when you do them yourselves; others will have greater impact when you invite additional people to join you. As you begin each chapter, map out a schedule for yourselves, deciding how often and when you will need to meet, who should be invited, and so forth. Look ahead as well to see when you may want to involve the entire congregation in various activities. Those dates will need to be put on the congregation's calendar so that everyone can plan for them.

Each exercise is followed by two additional steps. The first is called "Share Your Work." The committee should report often and by every available means. You may hold open meetings, write for the church newsletter, invite others to help, suggest that stories from your experiences make their way into sermons and pastoral prayers, give testimonies, or make announcements. You will be invited to produce maps and timelines that can be annotated with news clippings, photos, and other materials that will help others visualize what you are learning. Claim a conspicuous location for the products of your work so that interested members of the congregation can follow your progress.

Part of the task group's leadership is to help the members of the congregation enjoy discovering how much they already know as they imagine themselves into a new or renewed ministry. The information you present should be as much visual as conceptual, more dramatic than passive, more challenging than comforting, as much discussed as printed. Remember, your task is to break into deeply ingrained (sometimes unconscious) habits of mind and spirit, to let the impact of external change break into the congregation's consciousness.

The exercise is not complete, however, without *reflection* on what you have learned. In spite of what some people say, the facts do not speak for themselves. The facts the committee gathers are significant only as you take time to think hard about what they mean to you and to pray hard about what God might be saying to the congregation. We offer suggestions for questions you might ask yourselves or ways you might seek wisdom and insight in this process, but the reflection you do should be shaped by your own spiritual traditions. Find the biblical stories that can be ongoing touchstones for you and the practices of prayer that can call you into this risky territory. The committee needs to use its organizational skills to keep the process moving forward, but it also needs to make a spiritual commitment to engage the process at its deepest levels.

As you move into the work described in the final chapter of this workbook, the committee will need to undertake a new mode of planning, management, and oversight. At that point, you should be ready to begin handing off tasks to others who have caught the vision. The core committee will still have a critical role to play. As you think about how to foster new habits in your congregation's life, however, your work will consciously move outside the committee room, helping your emerging congregation to find a common life together. Even though many other groups will now take on responsibility for the new things that are happening, the planning team should maintain a regular schedule of meetings to assess how the congregation is doing, to monitor problem areas, and to implement new suggestions for easing the work of change. Having helped your congregation find its way through the wilderness, your role as continuing guides will be important.

We cannot tell you exactly where this journey will lead. We have attempted to provide some survival skills and strategies for forging your path. Even if neither the destination nor the map is yet clear to you, it is now time, in the grace of God, to venture forth. That, after all, is what a wilderness journey is all about.

Suggestions for Further Reading

1. James Hudnut Beumler's *Looking for God in the Suburbs* (New Brunswick, N.J.: Rutgers University Press, 1994) is an interesting account of the challenges facing suburban churches.

2. The changing relationship between families and churches is explored in Penny Long Marler's "Lost in the Fifties: The Changing Family and the Nostalgic Church," in *Work, Family, and Religion in Contemporary Society*, ed. Nancy T. Ammerman and Wade Clark Roof (New York: Routledge, 1995).

3. Nancy Eiesland writes about the challenges facing exurban congregations in *A Particular Place: Urban Restructuring and Religious Ecology* (New Brunswick, N.J.: Rutgers University Press, 2000).

4. The communities in this study of change and the responses of congregations in the communities are described in Nancy T. Ammerman, *Congregation and Community* (New Brunswick, N.J.: Rutgers University Press, 1997).

5. Recent surveys of U.S. congregations have found high numbers of recently founded congregations. See, for example, "Faith Communities Today," available at www.fact.hartsem.edu.

6. Carl S. Dudley, *Basic Steps Toward Community Ministries* (Washington, D.C.: Alban Institute, 1991), and Ammerman, *Congregation and Community.*

7. Among the Web sites you may find helpful are the Hartford Institute for Religion Research (www.hartfordinstitute.org); the comprehensive listing of sites related to church life found at www.religiousresources.org; the site cosponsored by the Alban

Institute, the Indianapolis Center for Congregations, and the Lilly Endowment (www.congregationalresources.org); or the more general resources and conversation to be found at www.religion-online.org or www.adherents.com.

8. Nancy T. Ammerman, Jackson W. Carroll, Carl S. Dudley, and William McKinney, eds., *Studying Congregations: A New Handbook* (Nashville, Tenn.: Abingdon Press, 1998).

CHAPTER TWO

GETTING THE LAY OF THE LAND

While they were in the wilderness and again when they reached the brink of the Jordan, the people of Israel had to figure out just where they were, what might lie ahead, and what resources they could find to sustain them. They had to learn to eat manna and to find water in unexpected places. In the beginning, they were disoriented by the wilderness, but God showed them how to survive in their new terrain. Of course, in the biblical story, they never quit complaining, but complaining served at least two important functions: it named the tensions they felt and it kept their life juices flowing freely.

The purpose of community mapping is to help the congregation locate itself in the wilderness, to name the tensions that members are feeling, and to keep the congregation's life juices flowing. Because seeing your terrain will help you make the most of its contours, the committee is invited to develop three kinds of maps. Although each of these maps could be completed in a few days, you should take your time, select your tools of analysis, and be sure to keep the congregation well informed and involved. Approach all of the exercises in this chapter as opportunities to learn more about your community and to open new possibilities for ministry. Rather than rushing to complete the task, block out several weeks or even an entire season—such as the fall or the spring—to enjoy and absorb your discoveries.

The three suggested maps are especially helpful for congregations that have lost their sense of place in the changing world. The first we call a *Place Map*, for designating the area that your members consider "your place." The second is a *People Map*, for identifying the populations who share this place with you. The development of this map will be supplemented by *conversations with community people.* The third map is an *Institutional Map* that will set your congregation in the context of major community events and institutions that have carried the people of this place through the years. Finally, we recommend that the committee consolidate its learning with a *Windshield Survey* that will help your congregation visualize community changes and possible opportunities for ministry.

Each map results in new discoveries. In the first, we ask you to name your assumptions and to define your boundaries. In the second map, we encourage you to look again at the different people who live and work in your space. And in the third, you will see the physical structures and institutions that have been the backbone of your community over time. The distinctive information on each separate map will continue to guide the congregation's thinking throughout its transition in ministry.

Because the purpose of this process is to understand community change, each map will include a glimpse of the past, a picture of the present, and a glimmer of the possible future. We suggest that you begin each exercise with your own memories and experiences, then include other people and sources of information, always pushing toward implications for the renewal of the congregation's ministry.

THE PLACE MAP: DEFINE YOUR BOUNDARIES

Background and Rationale

Mapmaking shapes the mind. In making this map, you will become aware of both geography and history. The exercise will push you from the past into the present. By putting your observations on paper, as a committee you will realize how often all of us impose the past on the present, and how much things have changed since you last looked carefully. Mapping provides a wake-up call to see the world the way it is.

But mapping does more than change your mind-set; it also brings you together as a working group. In constructing maps, members of the committee begin to see the world differently. We all have different priorities as we observe, we remember different events, and we recall the same events differently—we see with different eyes. By constructing a map together, you will pool your various perspectives and build an inclusive view of the strengths of your differences. What one congregation called "group think" will become an arena for exploring differences.

Further, maps are important as visual symbols for engaging the whole congregation in the journey of faith. As the committee places its large working maps where the congregation gathers, the maps will attract attention, give members a sense of belonging, and provide a constant reminder of the larger world in which the church is called to ministry. As they have for others, these maps can focus and energize your congregation's ministry.

Therefore, mapmaking should be a social event, with many excursions into other sources to check the accuracy of your findings. The work should be done on a sheet of paper large enough to allow the entire working group to see your progress and make suggestions as you work. Avoid being driven by perfection in detail, but try to create an appealing representation of your community. You should not produce a product so finished that you could not scrap it and start over if you discovered a major new insight. You may need several smaller maps to represent various interesting aspects of your community. Your primary task is to see the community clearly within the dynamics of change and to help both the church and the community to see themselves.

What to Do

To construct your Place Map, start where you are and with what you know. As the product of a group process, your map needs to be large enough for all participants to share in its construction, although often only one person at a time enters information. Create your map on a blank sheet of newsprint or butcher-block paper (not a printed map) attached to a wall and large enough (maybe three feet square or larger) to be seen from a distance by the committee and congregation.

Create a Basic Map Begin by situating your church building on the map, usually near the center so you can draw around it the primary streets and highways where your members live and that they travel when they come to church—the routes with which they are most familiar.[1] Next, as a framework for your thinking, identify major landmarks, such as highways, railway tracks, and primary streets (not necessarily every street), and natural barriers, such as hills, valleys, and rivers. For additional details, consult printed maps and drive around to remind yourselves of your terrain.

As soon as you begin, you will recognize that mapmaking requires choices (see Figure 2.1). Typically, committees have trouble agreeing on boundaries—and that is where learning begins.

Many congregations remember a time when the members lived in the geographical community where the church was located. Sometimes the church and the community were synonymous. But economic, social, and religious mobility have shattered such simplicity, and congregations organized more recently are apt to assume that they must draw from a larger area.

FIGURE 2.1   Mapmaking Requires Choices

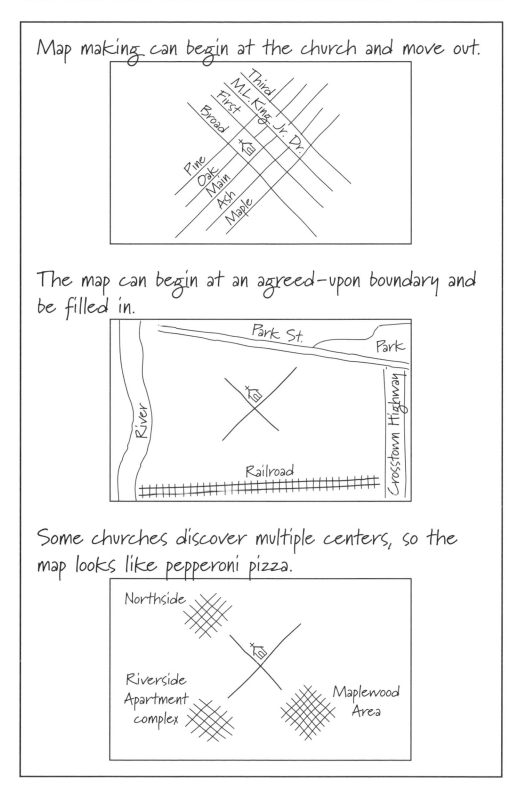

Map making can begin at the church and move out.

The map can begin at an agreed-upon boundary and be filled in.

Some churches discover multiple centers, so the map looks like pepperoni pizza.

There are many ways in which the relationship between a congregation and its community can change and be redefined.[2] The members of some older congregations have moved to new neighborhoods but continue to support the church in their old neighborhood. Churches whose members have been dispersed beyond a single neighborhood have become concerned for the larger area where their members live. Other churches have gained a reputation for a particular theological perspective or program emphasis, so they have attracted members who travel significant distances because they identify with the church's causes, programs, or beliefs, whether or not they feel an affinity with the church's immediate surrounding neighborhood.

Mapmaking forces a discussion and results in a choice. Most churches can identify the neighborhood in which they are located, where they may provide a variety of services. Some Protestants, like Catholics, call this area their "parish" and the larger region their "community," but there is no consistency in this usage. Even for Roman Catholics, the meaning of *parish* has changed significantly in recent years.[3] Religious traditions cannot provide a definitive answer about the boundaries of your functioning community. Your own careful discussion and sense of spiritual direction must be your guide.

The boundaries you set may not include all the places where your members are now scattered, but they should reflect the particular location where you believe God is calling you to ministry. These boundaries are not absolute or fixed for all time, but they are important for congregational consciousness. As a basis for helping your congregation deal with ministry in a changing time, you should openly discuss the reasons that various boundaries might be chosen and determine what you mean by the congregation's "community." It is this community that you will envision as you work through the rest of the exercises in this workbook. It may extend well beyond the immediate neighborhood of your church building. It is the part of the "social ecology" (the territory and people) of the region you identify as your spiritual territory.[4]

Process note: While this map is still relatively uncluttered with information, make two or more copies that show the major features of your area. You can use these copies later as the basis for your maps of people and institutions. Some groups short-cut the process (but lose some of the impact) by combining all the information on a single map, perhaps using different colors for institutions and populations. As you will soon discover, however, there is a great deal of information to be added to each map. Having several copies of the basic outline available will be an advantage.

Locate Your Members   Once you have agreed on the basic streets and boundaries of your Place Map, you need to locate where your members live in relation to the church building. Some congregations will mark the address of every member, others will cluster the homes of members into neighborhoods or ZIP code areas, and still others will indicate only the general direction from the church where members live with arrows pointing off the map. Your purpose is not detailed accuracy (although members will want to find themselves on the map) but to show the participation of members living in various areas relative to the church building.

One way to get a picture of the residential patterns of your congregation and how they have changed is to use push pins of different colors for the different eras in your church's history. Green might represent those who have been members longest, red those in the middle, and blue the newest members. When communities go through especially rapid growth or change, even people who live near each other may see the community around them in different ways. Nancy Eiesland found that within one exurban town some long-time residents were still locally oriented while newcomers saw the town as one part of a much bigger region.[5]

See if you can gather photos of members who live in various parts of the community. These should be posted beside your Place Map and connected to the members' geographical locations by string or yarn to give both color and interest to your map. Some congregations will need two Place Maps, one of a very large region to show how members are scattered, another of the smaller neighborhood where the congregation takes a special interest in providing services. But the purpose remains the same—to name the place of your ministry and to anchor your church's ministry in the "real world."

Share Your Work

Post your basic map in an accessible place and attach a brief interpretation for interested church members. Encourage discussion throughout the congregation about the boundaries and communities the committee has identified. Conversations are likely to be more natural if the map is posted in a commonly used entryway or where members customarily gather for coffee and small talk. But you should also be inventive in stirring up interest. You can do this through typical channels of information, such as the church's newsletter, the pastor's sermons, and classes, but you can also let the congregation know you care through testimonies about your experiences, prayer requests for the community you have identified, and special events that highlight your discoveries.

Reflection

Maps can inform your committee about your past and present, and suggest trajectories into the future. Are new members likely to come from different neighborhoods? What do you know about where older members *used* to live? Without a visual awareness of the community, churches tend to "float" without a sense of touching the ground in a time or place. Let your imaginations explore how you might use your Place Map to help other members of the congregation to feel more grounded. Simply by seeing the map and visualizing the community, the congregation will begin to engage with one another in a fresh way, thinking and talking about what it means to be a church in this place and at this time. As you continue through this mapping exercise, how can you help the congregation to be in touch in a tangible way with its place of ministry? How can you help the members to express their feelings about the changes they have seen in the streets and homes of the surrounding community? Any communal activity, from personal prayers to major parties, that you can undertake in the shadow of your Place Map will help lay the foundation for a future ministry that has its collective feet on the ground.

THE PEOPLE MAP: NAMING AND KNOWING YOUR NEIGHBORS

Background and Rationale

Every geographical area includes a variety of people who differ in age, gender, lifestyle, and status in the community. Some areas also embrace groups of people who differ in their nation of origin, racial-ethnic background, and cultural character. Sometimes these differences place barriers between people, and sometimes they make possible creative synergies.

The purpose of this exercise is to help your congregation better understand and make connections with the variety of people who live in your community. Some of these people may be future members of the congregation or allies in a common ministry. Conversely, some of these people may actively oppose a program you are promoting. For these and many other reasons, getting acquainted with the people who live and work within the bounds of the church's community is essential to thinking about the ministry to which you are called.

What to Do

We suggest that you create a *People Map,* recognizing that such maps are never finished. The People Map should be interesting, dynamic, and more suggestive than definitive. We encourage you to use several sources to create your map, including your current perceptions, statistical reports, contacts made through members of your congregation, and perhaps most challenging, conversations with neighbors you don't yet know.

Make a List   Beginning with the committee members' own perceptions and assumptions, name the population groups who live or work in your community (see Figure 2.2). Some groups may be defined by a strong commitment to a religious tradition. For instance, are there neighborhoods in your community that are distinctively Jewish or Catholic? Some groups are defined by a distinctive language or culture. For example, are there pockets of Polish speakers or large Spanish-speaking districts? Some groups are committed to a particular lifestyle. For instance, are there neighborhoods where artists or gay and lesbian people live? Some groups are defined by economic status. For example, are there businesses and housing that attract people with low incomes? Are other sections of the community designed for high-income households? Some groups are defined by age and life cycle. For instance, where do the older citizens live? Where are the young families, young singles, and single-parent families? Do the teenagers gather in particular places? Do the elderly cluster for food and fellowship? (You can use the "Working Notes: Who Shares Our Community" to make your own preliminary list.)

Most communities include a mix of people with various characteristics, and some groups are not easily pinned down to a particular location. Even individuals who are not concentrated in a certain area can recognize an affinity for each other in such groups as young mothers, elderly singles, or immigrants with a common culture. As they communicate with one another, these neighbors create the networks of association that strengthen the fabric of your neighborhood.[6]

While making the list, the committee needs to create a safe space in the conversation where members can share their memories and experiences, their priorities and prejudices. While you need to acknowledge your own unconscious stereotypes and ignorance (you cannot know all other groups as well as your own), you should also try to uncover some of the popular wisdom and community perceptions of who lives where.

FIGURE 2.2 People Who Live in Our Neighborhood

- Families with school-age children
- Schools with various reputations
- Single-parent families—Is there a network?
- Thai immigrant families and food store
- Single older adults, living alone
- Empty nesters
- Gay and lesbian couples
- Cultural arts supporters (music and drama)
- Lower- and moderate-income families
- Teenagers looking for something to do
- Educators, lawyers, and other professionals
- Students, especially in local law school
- Long-term residents and recent arrivals
- Taxpayers frustrated with city government

WORKING NOTES:
Who Shares Our Community?

From your own personal experience with the community you have identified, what concentrations of people are part of this community?

Are there language groups?

Are there distinct religious groups (including people of no faith)?

Are there different income and social-class groups?

Are there groups identified by need or lifestyle?

Are there other important groupings?

If the church is located in a community that has recently experienced significant social change, and if the committee has reached a level of open communication, this exercise is apt to be emotional, perhaps even explosive. It is good to recognize the feelings that change and diversity can arouse. The more familiar the members are with the area, the more likely it is that they will see things differently. Describing the church's neighbors may be a difficult and painful exercise. Be sure to allow time to reflect on your feelings in the spiritual practices your group has adopted.

Make a Preliminary Draft   On a clean copy of the Place Map the group created earlier, locate the significant groups of people who share your space. Your task in developing the People Map is to highlight the diversity of people who inhabit your community while at the same time providing both the committee and the congregation with the confidence that they can make connections with these people and possibly build a future in ministry together.

You have already named some of these people on your list of population groups. Now enter them on your People Map. You may use lines and arrows to locate groups or to indicate the connections between groups. What are the popular designations for particular blocks and what informal names are used in the neighborhoods but rarely appear on official maps? Groups that are not easily located can remain on a list posted beside the map. The People Map need not be accurate in every detail, but it should increase the congregation's awareness of various populations that share its place.

Get the Data   After the committee has attempted to draw the map from its members' memories and impressions, it is time to add a measure of statistical objectivity and historical depth. This information should affirm some expectations and challenge others, and it may often add details on unseen newcomers. Numerous resources exist to help identify the distribution of population groups in your community. Community planning offices are often helpful. You can also retrieve information from the U.S. Census Bureau (see Table 2.1), the local library, and reports from real estate or school officials.[7] Your denomination may also be able to help you obtain the information you need, and there are commercial consulting firms that supply demographic profiles to churches.[8] The gap between your expectations and this more objective information should increase the committee's awareness of the changing community and of new potentials for ministry. Your committee's growing firsthand knowledge of the community may also fill in gaps that exist in the statistical data others have collected.

With this additional information, complete a preliminary draft of your People Map. As the committee reaches consensus about the major population groups in the area, enter the names of those groups on the map in their general areas of work and residence. Use a variety of dashes, dotted lines, and bright colors to make your map interesting. Especially mark groups that have energy and are expanding and those that have special needs, such as the marginalized populations that might shape your ministry in this place.

Table 2.1
A Demographic Profile of Our Neighborhood,
from 2000 Census Data

Total population	8,464	*Household income*	
Ethnicity		Less than $15,000	24.5%
White (not Hispanic)	61.2%	$15,000–$34,999	35.9%
Black (not Hispanic)	21.3%	$35,000–$74,999	28.1%
Hispanic	14.8%	$75,000 or more	11.5%
Other	2.8%	Persons living below the	
Median age	32.5 years	poverty line	11.0%
Education (adults 25		Families living below the	
or older)		poverty line	7.1%
Less than high school		*Persons per household*	1.94
diploma	20%	*"Linguistically isolated"*	
High school diploma		*households* (where no one	
or some college	40%	speaks English)	345
Bachelor's degree		*Unemployment rate*	
or more	40%	Neighborhood	6.45%
		Citywide	10.73%

Make the Connections   Now that you have gathered the statistical information, enter your congregation's connections to the various groups identified on your People Map. This can be done in many ways. For example, note on the map where your members live or work in comparison to where they once lived and worked. What connections to community people have been made or lost? In addition, locate the gathering places where the church has contact with the community, if only in passing, such as cultural clubs, issue groups, community agencies, schools, recreation areas, and the like. Most congregations discover that they have far more real and potential points of contact with community groups than they previously recognized.

Share Your Work

Both the list of people who live in your neighborhood and the People Map should be open to additional entries as you continue to gather information. Many groups noted on the list will be scattered across the map rather than clustered in a particular location. As you work with the list and map, keep both posted together where the members of the congregation can share your continuing inquiry. Some congregations have used this place for an open meeting with church members to hear their impressions of how the population has changed as they have lived in the community.

CONVERSATIONS WITH COMMUNITY PEOPLE

Background and Rationale

After the committee has polished the list of population groups and the map and has noted the points of contact between the congregation and the community, its members should begin interviewing people in the community. These conversations should become part of each exercise you do in the community and within the congregation. Wide-ranging conversations are basic to completing the maps and ultimately to developing the church's new expressions of ministry. Such dialogue should be a Christian commitment, a life-long habit, not just another activity.

Interviews are an exercise of self-disinterest and humility. This is not a moment to evangelize for the faith, nor is it a time to sell the various programs of the church—although these are worthy ambitions under other conditions. Interviews are different. They are opportunities for listening, which is key to the difficult task of understanding how someone else experiences your community differently.

Interviews require the discipline of "active listening," the skill of getting inside the logic of the speaker with questions and discussion until you can accurately record in a few words how that person approaches an area of common concern. Interviews are important throughout your efforts to understand and relate to your community (and to understand your own congregation).

What to Do

On the basis of the list and the People Map, the committee should choose people to interview who represent the range of those who live and work in the community (see Figure 2.3). Because you cannot talk with everyone, be intentional about your choices. First, connections count: start your conversations with people who are already known by members of your existing congregation. Follow the yarn on your Place Map to old neighbors and other contacts you already have. Second, try to locate people who can provide the long view of community change—the hairdresser who has kept shop for forty years, the retired school principal, the newspaper reporter with a community beat. Select others to represent various populations, especially groups you might want to highlight in your new ministries. (You can use the "Working Notes: Preparing for Community Interviews" to plan your interview strategy.) Approach each conversation

FIGURE 2.3 Conversations in the
Community: Whom Should We Interview?

Educators: principal, teachers, staff
Political leaders: elected officials or their staff
Community planners: ask for maps and so on
Social service agencies: staff and clients
Police commanders, cops on the beat
Business leaders and local shopkeepers
News reporters for television and press
Clinic and nursing home staff
Families, youth, children
Bartender, laundromat user

as an interested listener who cares for the community and who needs to learn the particular perspective this person (or group) can offer.

Focus Determine ahead of time what sorts of questions you want to ask. For example, you might begin with a general question about where your community has been and where it is going. But also ask what the most critical needs are, where the greatest assets are to be found, and other questions the committee decides are crucial. After each interview, be sure to note any follow-up that might be appropriate, who will do it, and when.

WORKING NOTES:
Preparing for Community Interviews

List here the persons you will talk with to learn more about the community you have identified as your church's desired ministry area. Remember that these are people who are not members of your congregation but represent the diversity of people and concerns in your community.

Begin with those with whom your own church members have direct connections.

Neighbor to be interviewed   Who can introduce you?

_____   _____

_____   _____

_____   _____

_____   _____

Add other new contacts you will make (individuals, offices, and agencies, such as school principals or community service organizations).

Neighbor to be interviewed   Location and contact information

_____   _____

_____   _____

_____   _____

_____   _____

Add places where you might naturally talk with people (laundromat, bus stop, park or playground).

Review your list to include contacts who might represent community differences in age, family size, lifestyle, job, racial or ethnic background, and so on. Rank your contacts, starting where you are most comfortable.

Plan your questions. You might begin with these:

- When did you come to the area and why?

- What are the most important trends and changes, and are they good or not?

- What's best about this community? What needs to be changed?

You might end by asking:

- Who else would you suggest that we contact?

Enjoy the conversation. Don't be limited by your planned questions. And don't forget to ask for permission to report what each person has said.

Keep Records   Making a record of an interview so you can share it later is difficult.[9] Most of the congregations we studied agreed that, compared to all of the material they gathered in their community studies, the interviews were the hardest to capture in print. In these interactive experiences, body language and feeling tones intersect with spoken words to make a whole impression that cannot be reduced to words, pictures, or even video (although all are helpful). Be sure that you take good notes both during and immediately after the conversation. You might begin by recording your experience on the "Working Notes: Remembering Your Interviews." Then you can summarize a few key themes on a card or piece of paper that can later be added to the map (when available, a photo is helpful) (see Figure 2.4). Despite their illusive character, these interviews can be a magnificent window for the whole congregation to rediscover its connections with the community by recognizing all that its members have in common with people who are not members. Remember, however, to respect the privacy of those you interview by requesting their permission to share content from the interview with your congregation.

Summarize Themes   List the issues that were discussed in your interviews and the views that were expressed (see Figure 2.5). Note especially those items that affirm your current ministry or suggest new areas of caring. There is no reason to make these reports into literary gems—a list of key words is all that is necessary, and a sense of the ministries that these words imply. (*Note:* You will want to remember what these community members said about change in the community so you can use it to create the timeline in the next chapter.)

Add Notes to Your People Map   What do these conversations add to your understanding of who shares your community? Go back to your People Map and add notes to what you have already discovered. You might connect some of your interview summaries with yarn to specific groups and areas you have identified on the map.

WORKING NOTES:
Remembering Your Interviews

You can use a page like this to make notes after each of your community interviews.

Person visited:

Date and place:

New information and insight about the community:

Person's primary concerns:

My personal response:

Positive and negative implications for our ministry:

Do we have permission to share what this person said?
Any limitations?

Follow-up (prayer and actions needed):

FIGURE 2.4   Interview Summary

JESSIE SMITH

Lives in Eden Nursing Home, age 87

- Takes a walk every day
- Misses the old neighborhood shopping
- Thinks people drive too fast on her street
- Knows our pastor but not our members
- Says, "Kids have it easy these days, but the parents—no, sir, I wouldn't want to do that again."

(Attach photograph, if available.)

FIGURE 2.5   Interview Themes

Other institutions that share our concerns:
Neighboring congregation
Local library and school
Boys and girls clubs

Biggest economic impact:
Engine factory
Military base
Community college

The gathering places:
Sports park
Local pub

Biggest change looming:
New highway coming through

Share Your Work

Your congregation needs to know that contact was made with community people who "care like we do." If you have obtained permission from those you interviewed, post summaries of the themes from your conversations with the maps you have been sharing with the congregation. Church members are often fascinated by the committee's choice of people to interview and the topics covered. The posted summaries can be simple yet attractive, including the name, social location, and, if possible, a picture of the person you interviewed. List the topics you talked about and highlight a brief quote (fifty words or less) that helps your members catch the spirit of the conversation. Because the person interviewed may be known by others in the congregation, write your comments in such a way that others might be encouraged to continue that conversation.

Post your People Map along with the list of population groups and the interviews in a conspicuous space that invites conversation. Make clear (with pictures, yarn, drawings, and the like) the working connections the congregation has with individuals or groups in the community. Also post photos obtained from others in the congregation that show members enjoying good times in old familiar places and that reflect past experiences in particular neighborhood groups. Some of these artifacts and memorabilia can be incorporated into worship events, lifted up in the children's sermon, and made the focal point for committee and congregational prayer. The People Map should be an earthy (sometimes messy) expression of the roots the congregation shares with the citizens of the community.

Reflection

These listing, mapping, and interviewing exercises can inform your social analysis and spiritual sensitivity at several levels. They can provide a mass of information about the changes that community residents and leaders have experienced and about the lifestyles of cultural groups in different parts of the community. For those who are feeling displaced by recent changes, these activities can provide an arena of spiritual therapy to exorcise bad memories that might poison future efforts. They can also reveal personal connections between the congregation and various cultural groups that are now a part of the community.

Personal interviews will put a face on the problems you discover in your community studies. Through these conversations you will learn more than facts about the community. You will also learn the complexity of the issues and find allies in shared concerns. Over time, you may weave together a network of people who are sustained by the same God, who care about many of the same issues you do, and who learn to work together even when they do not always agree.

Explore the impact that interviewing individuals and developing a People Map have had on spiritual awareness in both the congregation and the community. At this point, many congregations discover a loop of increased self-confidence: when the church shows interest in the community, others in the community accept the church as a partner, and church leaders begin to think and act in more inclusive ways. In the process, church members can feel a sense of renewal, that God will sustain them even as they risk reaching out to others in new ways.

THE INSTITUTIONAL MAP: RECOGNIZING HISTORICAL RESOURCES

Background and Rationale

As time passes, every community creates a wide variety of institutions and agencies for cooperative activities ranging from common interests among a few people to the determined will of the larger community. Churches often place so much emphasis on individual people and human relationships that they neglect or overlook the importance of the organizations and associations through which people join in common action. These institutions provide forums in which we as both Christians and citizens can review our situation, assemble resources, make decisions, keep records, and carry on the business of living.

In this exercise, you are asked to identify the various institutions, agencies, and associations that have developed over the years in your community. These organizations express very different aspects of community life: business and manufacturing, education and the arts, government and public welfare, social and cultural life, and of course religious commitments. Your study should concentrate on institutions that have had a major impact on the whole community and those that share the concerns of your congregation.

In this mapping exercise, you will locate your congregation in the midst of other institutions in your area. (You might begin by compiling your personal knowledge on the "Working Notes: Important Community Institutions.") Some of these institutions are your partners and allies in caring for the community, others are your competition or opposition in developing your ministry. By recognizing these institutions, your congregation will also discover something about itself.

What to Do

We invite you to make an *Institutional Map* of your community. Because churches are inclined to think in terms of personal relationships, the challenge of this exercise is to keep the focus on institutions. Look especially for two sorts: the larger institutions that cast their shadow across the whole community, and the smaller ones that are important to you because they share some of your basic values and commitments.

Make a List   Begin with free association. List the groups that come immediately to mind in response to the question, "What are your important community institutions?" Record the list on newsprint and then look

WORKING NOTES:
Important Community Institutions

Before your task group meets, use your own personal knowledge to make notes about the important institutions in your community.

Large employers and industries that influence the community	Assets and interests I associate with this employer or industry
Popular gathering places in the community	Who comes and why
Organizations with which our congregation works	Special contributions this organization makes

more closely at your responses. Is there a major employer (such as a large hospital) or significant industry (such as a car assembly plant) that dominates the life of your community? Note broad social and economic movements that have had an impact in your community (such as the civil rights movement). Also note the smaller institutions that influence the social and cultural community. Pay special attention to institutions that share your values in education, family life, health, recreation, music and the arts, care of the elderly, and so on. Be sure to list all of the religious institutions, even if you do not feel closely allied with them. Finally, add another important "institution": the places where people gather and that encourage communication among segments of the community, such as pubs, sports clubs, laundromats, restaurants, cultural centers, parks and playgrounds, and popular stores where some groups simply "hang out." Through further discussion, expand and refine your list. You may also want to organize it around particular themes.

Create the Map   With your institutional list clearly in view, use one of the unused Place Maps that you set aside during the first mapping exercise to develop your Institutional Map. Begin by defining different ways the land is used: Where are the shopping areas? The large employers? Where are the governmental agencies—from town hall to the libraries, from schools and playgrounds to parks and public spaces? When you have gleaned what you can from your own memories, consult previously existing maps, such as the general maps that can be found in your city's or county's planning office, promotional maps provided by the chamber of commerce or visitors center (some humorous, some highly distorted), or specialized maps developed by schools, highway departments, and utility companies. With your maps in hand, take a walk or ride around your neighborhood to see for yourselves.

Exercise your curiosity: Where are different forms of housing—the apartments, the private homes—located in your community and what is on the margins between them? Where do people work? What are the industries, and where are the major businesses? Where do people express their interests? Where are the libraries, cultural centers, religious centers, and other places where people gather?[10]

Choose from all this information the most significant items to enter on your Institutional Map. Mark particularly the social agencies that share your concern for the people of the community, such as the neighborhood school, community center, social security office, library, police station, courts, and the like. You may also want to include other historic institutions, such as large employers, civic and cultural centers, and major gathering places. Marking the roads and walkways that members use most often can give a feeling of how people enter and exit the community.

Annotate and Illustrate   Some congregations have worked hard to incorporate the historical perspective into their maps. They have enriched the two-dimensional Institutional Map with historical depth by using colors and lines to mark the comings and goings of institutions. For example, you can use a bright color (perhaps red) to identify the energy of new and growing institutions, such as a vibrant storefront church, a local gathering place for young adults, or a sports field that is in constant use. You can use solid lines to draw institutions that already exist and broken lines to show where new institutions plan to locate. Colors and lines can also mark the decline and disappearance of gone-but-not-forgotten community institutions. Use dark (perhaps shaded black) dotted lines to recall institutions that are no longer part of the community. If committee members have a sense of historical drama, you may want to make a separate "ghost map" that shows the shadows of institutions that have departed, etching the memory of the old community.

Institutional Maps will attract more attention if decorated with additional information. You can add interest by attaching photographs of community buildings and activities, from both recent events and the more distant past. Every congregation has members who have photos of the community "the way it used to be." Newspapers and libraries have an amazing "morgue" of old photos you can borrow. But do not be limited by old and outside resources. Use your own photographs to remind members of what they have seen, especially if you have old pictures that show how things have changed.

Make the Connections   Finally, note on your Institutional Map any partnerships or programs you share with other congregations or community institutions. Where possible, list the names of your members who are involved in these shared programs. You might use a piece of colored yarn to connect your building with those of other agencies, and a miniature banner or flag to identify the program and people involved. When you visually connect your church building with other churches or agencies in the community, you affirm the people and strengthen the programs.[11]

Share Your Work

Post your Institutional Map alongside the People Map and Place Map. Include a key to explain the various symbols you have used. Then arrange a time for a member of the committee to describe the map to a gathering of congregational members. This description should be a kind of community stewardship report, a discussion of the institutional resources in the community. Name the assets you have identified—generally many more than most members of the congregation have imagined. Invite members to add to or comment on your discoveries.

Reflection

Through the process of making the Institutional Map, the working group will become more aware of the role of the congregation among the groups that contribute to the community. What is the impact of seeing your congregation as one resource among others? Can you build bridges based on your common concerns yet retain your unique character and strength?

Explore the implications for your congregation's standing in the community. Have the people with whom you have had contact begun to think of the church as a potential partner in your areas of shared concern? Do they treat the church differently than they used to and include it in community meetings to which it has not been invited before? Have they visited the church to see your maps? Have you invited them and prepared for their visit?

Now consider your stewardship of the assets that God makes available in your community. Which of these institutions are especially important to the well-being of the community? Which provide critically needed services and do so especially well? What services are missing? Note especially the churches and other agencies with which you have worked, and those that are potential allies, partners, and resources in the development of new ministries.

SUMMARY EXERCISE: WINDSHIELD SURVEY

Background and Rationale

A Windshield Survey is an overview of the community that can be used to involve the rest of the members of your congregation in the study process. Many of them know that change is happening "out there," but it is not real to them until they make personal contact with it. The Windshield Survey is an activity in which the members can see, and even touch, what is happening in the community not as a threat but as an opportunity for renewal in ministry.[12]

What to Do

Your Windshield Survey will challenge the congregation to look anew at its once familiar community. As the members explore what the committee has organized, they can add new dimensions that you may have missed. Using the wall-sized Place Map as a guide, produce copies of a small Windshield Map on pieces of 8½-by-11-inch paper, including drawings and notations that call attention to community changes that the committee feels signal opportunities for ministry. Note a few of the significant changes that were recorded on the various maps. You might prepare your list by using the "Working Notes: Reflections on Community Change" as a starting point. For each key change, trend, or discovery, select one place in the community where it can most clearly be seen. Mark that place on the Windshield Survey map so that members can explore the territory, but invite each participant to add notes about other changes they see.

You might also do the Windshield Survey as a game, like a treasure hunt that challenges members to name old places that are now gone, or like a scavenger hunt, in which members locate objects and symbols of community transition (see Figure 2.6). Your task is to get the members' attention and challenge them to "see again for the first time" the places, people, and institutions of their community.

Leave a stack of Windshield Maps where members can pick them up. Ask them to note on these maps any changes they have observed and their associated feelings, then find ways to share these responses. Post on a wall with your other materials the finished maps of members who have tried the treasure hunt for old buildings or the scavenger hunt for hidden symbols of community change. Encourage members to use old community contacts or simply to ask the people they meet to help them understand "the changes around here." The only real experts on the community are the community members themselves. Encourage everyone in the congregation to make at least one contact in the community and enter their impressions on their map, then post the maps (or other notes) for all to see.

WORKING NOTES:
Reflections on Community Change

What are the foundations of this community—the things that never change or the interests and concerns that bring people together?

What are the changes and trends you expected?

What are changes or trends that have surprised you so far?

What difference do these changes make?

Why are they important to you? To your church?

Additional notes and comments to be shared with the committee:

Follow-up prayer concerns and suggested actions:

FIGURE 2.6 Windshield Survey:
Community Treasure Hunt

Match the numbered items with the correct letter on the neighborhood map.

1. Senior citizen home with oldest resident
2. Trolley tracks (now covered)
3. Largest business (by dollar volume)
4. Oldest home built (date) and most recent home (date)
5. Most apartments in one building
6. Place teenagers like to gather
7. Grade school with the most new students
8. Twenty-four-hour emergency health care

Add your notes to the community maps already posted in the Fellowship Hall.

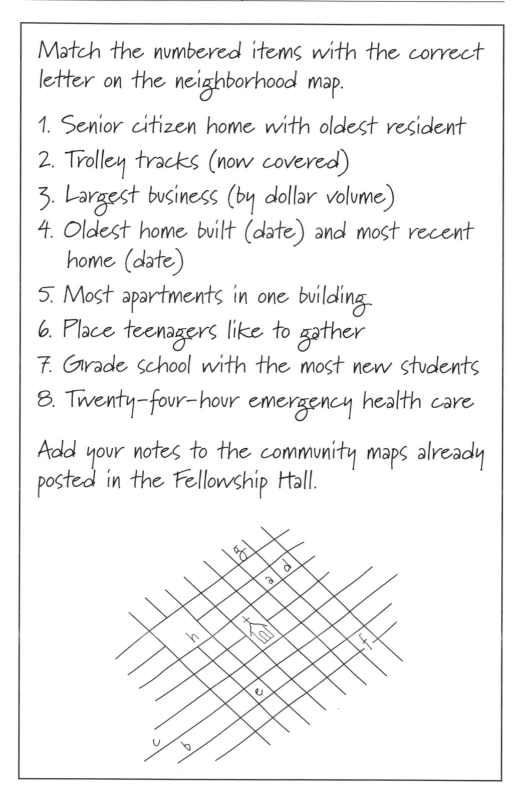

Share Your Work

You should now have several windows on the community—the Place Map, the Institutional Map, the People Map, interview summaries, and Windshield Surveys—all illustrated with pictures and news stories, and often including colored lines of yarn connecting the church with its community allies. Because this material may have been developed over several weeks or even months, schedule a particular time to post all of this handiwork in a specific area where it can receive maximum attention from the flow of congregational members.

The display itself can attract interest and generate support for ministry. If possible, invite former members to one or more special events and urge them to lend you pictures, news stories, and other memorabilia for your exhibition. You can also use this display as a centerpiece for a special event to which nonmembers from the community are invited. Inviting outstanding citizens who have moved away or current political figures can enhance your celebration. You might also add musical events or combine it with a religious celebration. Your history can be a gift to the whole community, as well as to the congregation.

Reflection

The Windshield Survey is more than a quick look at the community through the eyes of the planning committee. Making the committee's best wisdom vulnerable to challenge increases the likelihood that the congregation will claim ownership. This exercise should generate a kind of spiritual renewal through a combination of nostalgia and hope. Nostalgia can be therapeutic when members admit their sense of loss while also celebrating past joys. Hope comes from rediscovering the firm reality that all communities must from time to time be redefined, refreshed, and even reinvented.

These exercises can help identify the networks of personal relations and associations between the church and the community that are (or can become) a community's greatest asset by reflecting a complex tapestry of memories, friendships, institutions, and commitments that sustain community life. Awareness of these groups and their links to the congregation are treasured resources for ministry, past and future. No less than money does, these human and social resources call for stewardship that is informed by the Spirit.

SUMMARY

Community mapping provides a way for congregations to locate themselves within the constantly changing conditions of transitional communities. By using these maps, congregations can harness the energy of the restless tides and use the power that comes from change for constructive purposes. As these exercises reveal the community, congregations can look for the ripples and currents that invite their investment in new ministries.

These maps will help you identify place, people, and institutional resources that may help your congregation visualize in these community changes new opportunities to embody the Gospel in ministry. The most powerful use of this material is simply to ignite the imagination of your congregation. But to fully release those energies, you must help the congregation understand itself and claim its ministry more fully. That is the purpose of the next set of exercises.

Suggestions for Further Reading

1. An extended exploration of mapping congregational communities can be found in *Studying Congregations*, pp. 47–54.

2. The first chapter of Ammerman's *Congregation and Community* includes several case studies of dramatic and not-so-dramatic community changes, from immigration to plant closings to suburban growth. Reading about the communities she studied may provide your committee with insight into your own situation.

3. For an interesting historical look at Catholic parishes, see John McGreevy's *Parish Boundaries: The Catholic Encounter with Race in the Twentieth-Century Urban North* (Chicago: University of Chicago Press, 1996). Robert Orsi has edited a fascinating collection of more recent accounts of the relationship between religious groups and the urban places they occupy. See *Gods of the City* (Bloomington: Indiana University Press, 1999).

4. For a more extensive discussion of how congregations are situated in a social and cultural context, see "Ecology: Seeing the Congregation in Context," pp. 40–77 in *Studying Congregations.*

5. Nancy Eiesland, in *A Particular Place* (New Brunswick, N.J.: Rutgers University Press, 2000), describes the many ways different people and different congregations adapted to change that transformed a small rural town into an Atlanta exurb.

6. John Kretzmann and John L. McKnight have highlighted the informal associations and networks that sustain communities and provided useful guidelines for identifying these associations and networks as "community assets." See Kretzmann and McKnight, *Building Communities from the Inside Out* (Evanston, Ill.: Center for Urban Affairs, Northwestern University, 1993).

7. Further details on community demographic studies can be found in *Studying Congregations*, pp. 55–66.

8. Two companies that provide packages of demographic information for churches are Visions-Decisions, P.O. Box 94144, Atlanta, GA 30377 (www.visions-decisions.com), and Percept, 151 Kalmus Drive, Suite A104, Costa Mesa, CA 92626 (www.perceptnet.com/ pn4/address.htm). A good example of assistance from a denominational source is *Counting Your Community: A Video Workshop* by the Division for Congregational Ministries of the Evangelical Lutheran Church in America (ELCA), Chicago (undated). It includes links to ZIP code–level census reports available to ELCA congregations at www.elca.org or customized reports available by mail from ELCA's Department for Research and Evaluation. In addition, the Census Bureau's own site (www.census.gov) is increasingly user-friendly.

9. Helpful tips for interviewers can be found in *Studying Congregations*, pp. 203–208.

10. Carl Dudley has gathered information from twenty-five congregations who have identified their boundaries, anchor institutions, and gathering places as a basis for developing community ministry. See Carl S. Dudley, *Basic Steps Toward Community Ministry* (Washington, D.C.: Alban Institute, 1991).

11. For guidelines for gathering additional information about possible institutional allies, secular and religious, see *Studying Congregations*, pp. 71–74.

12. For further guidelines on taking a driving or walking "space tour," see *Studying Congregations*, pp. 47–50.

CHAPTER THREE

SIZING UP YOUR TABERNACLE

One of the most amazing things that happened on the long journey between Egypt and Jordan was that the people of Israel constructed a tabernacle. As a place of worship, the tabernacle symbolized who they were and how they were related to God—and that they were still on a journey. It was also a place constructed out of the particular gifts this group of people had to give. We are told in Exodus 25 that God said, "Tell the Israelites to set aside a contribution for me; you shall accept whatever contribution each shall freely offer . . . gold, silver, copper; violet, purple, and scarlet yarn; fine linen and goats' hair; tanned rams' skins. . . ." The list goes on. No less than that tabernacle, every congregation is made up of the gifts its people have brought to it over time, and each congregation is the unique creation made from those gifts.

The purpose of the exercises in this chapter is to give the congregation perspective on its current situation and the opportunity to practice the honest self-assessment we talked about in Chapter One. The method used is the construction of timelines to identify the strengths and limitations the members bring to this moment in the church's history. Maps and timelines provide different perspectives on similar situations. Maps offer a cross section of many elements at a particular moment in time, while timelines visualize the historical dynamics of a few elements over a more extended period. In this chapter, we move from community mapping to the construction of congregational timelines to gain new perspective on the church in its community context.

As in the exercise in community mapping, the timeline should be constructed in ways that will enable you to create displays and reports that invite conversation. Because the goal of these study activities is to inform and challenge the congregation, the committee should use every means available to encourage maximum participation. Like the maps, the congregational timelines should be enhanced with news clippings, photos, and other materials. They should be large and located in prominent places where interested members of the congregation can follow the committee's progress and perhaps join in the various exercises. The most powerful congregational and community studies are not the work of an exclusive committee but the shared activity of wide segments of the congregation. Report often and through every available means—such as open meetings, newsletters, and invitations to help—and incorporate the committee's findings into sermons, pastoral prayers, and informal conversations. Part of the committee's leadership is to help other members of the congregation enjoy the discoveries and affirmations through the process of imagining themselves into a new or renewed ministry.

History can be a rich resource for congregations in changing communities when it is used knowingly, but it is a liability when it uses us. Constructive use of historical memory offers ample evidence of crises that a congregation has successfully survived and does not permit the "golden age" to set false standards for the current era. History not only authorizes change, it mandates it. As an older parishioner once explained to a new pastor, "Those who say 'we always did it this way' are lying! We've always done it all sorts of ways." In the series of exercises presented in this chapter, we invite you to use your congregation's history as a resource for change, to explore together your past and to weave these facts, events, and stories together to explain the present and open new options for the future. Have fun, because rediscovering the past can energize a congregation, especially those who, like God, have a sense of humor about the incongruities of creation.

Using this chapter, your planning committee will create several multidimensional congregational timelines. You can begin with common memory, then add information until, at the end of the process, the timelines provide a comprehensive overview of the church's history through several windows. Most churches find that rarely is everyone interested in all of the strands on your timeline, but collectively these strands provide a complete tapestry of congregational character over time. Throughout these exercises, you can mix and match tasks and personnel, combining and expanding them as your interests dictate. Although each timeline might be completed at a single meeting, after perhaps a few hours of research, most church committees take several weeks to gather information and often use an extended event (such as a weekend retreat or family camp) to assemble and examine their findings. Creating these materials works best when the committee discovers and uses the diverse interests of its many members to develop, present, and absorb this fascinating story.

We invite you to develop a *Basic Timeline,* then to expand it with four timeline-related exercises, and finally to integrate them all in a summary and celebration event. Although the initial and summary exercises should be used in proper sequence, the others can be done in any order or all at the same time. Typically, different people take an interest in each area—buildings and facilities, leaders and decisions, physical and spiritual resources, worship and music—so consider dividing the tasks according to the interests of the committee members or other members of the congregation you can recruit to work with you.

Your task is to identify and celebrate the dynamics of change. You do not need to discover everything about the past, but in each area you should report on a few powerful symbols (events, artifacts, people of faith) to honor the congregation's journey and invite recommitment to the future.

To construct the Basic Timeline, begin by talking with a few old-timers, who can help the committee gain an overview of the church's history. This exercise will help you situate the congregation within a larger historical context, but your primary purpose will be to gain a working knowledge of the historical facts and of members' memories.

The *Buildings and Facilities Timeline* will tap the congregation's memories of its physical structures and artifacts. When were the buildings constructed? What were they built for? How have they been used over the years? When were they renovated? What is the current traffic of participants throughout the week?

The *Leadership and Decision-Making Timeline* will explore the roles played by particular leaders who have left their imprint (not always positive), as well as adding a picture of today's ways of accomplishing the church's work. Who are the well-remembered leaders? What were their accomplishments? How did they do it? What is their legacy? How do they compare with the present generation of leaders?

The *Resources Timeline* will help you chart the rise and fall of membership, finances, and spiritual vitality across the years. What is your historic profile and how does it compare with your present condition?

The *Worship and Music Timeline* will help you see that worship is a constantly rewoven fabric of faith. What worship styles and expressions have been used over the years? When were the contemporary styles of music, prayers, preaching, and the like first introduced in your worship? What are the pressures for change?

Finally, we invite you to have a *Summary Celebration.* Organize a major "happening" to use the information you have collected to develop a Comprehensive Timeline that reflects the church's journey and helps you discern where God is leading the congregation in the next chapter of its history. What have been the key mission emphases and central goals of the church over the years?

You may include in these exercises a variety of people from both the congregation and the larger community. We urge you not to rush the experience; rather, enjoy this time of discovery and sharing. Make clear to the participants your deep sense of respect for the information and feelings they share with you. Listen carefully, appreciating fully the years of experience they will bring to your inquiry.

While these exercises demand a thoughtful, verbal expression of your story, they also invite the exercise of your spiritual imagination and discernment. Throughout the process, pause regularly to notice God's presence in your midst. Where has God's hand been visible in your history, and where are God's gifts to you visible in the resources you now enjoy? You will need to depend on your faith to give you the courage to see yourselves honestly and the wisdom to see what sort of new tabernacle your gifts might make.

BASIC TIMELINE: AN ORIENTATION EXERCISE

Background and Rationale

An enjoyable yet powerful way to mobilize and unify a group, the time-line exercise is used in many organizational settings, from not-for-profit hospitals and social agencies to commercial businesses and competitive corporations.[1] The timeline can visually help you recall some of the significant events and trends that have shaped your congregation and its changing community. In the process, you can engage some of the current players to describe similar struggles and forces that still affect the present situation. Together you can begin to define possible future trends and directions that are unfolding.

Countless congregations have found this series of exercises to be the most revealing and energizing activities they have ever done. Working together to tell the significant stories in the congregation's history can provide vital insight into the values that have held it together and the visions that have kept it going. This initial timeline combines two objectives— to record the general history of your community and to tell the specific story of your congregation. Both goals are important, and the gathering of each history could be a separate event.[2]

For congregations faced with changing communities, developing historical consciousness is not a delightful distraction—rather, the task is crucial. This exercise represents both the resistance you face and your greatest resource in overcoming that barrier. To create a new future, congregations must break through the shortsighted assumptions of the present. They must see themselves as groups that have already changed over the years in response to evolving circumstances. This exercise to help break through the resistance is energizing and fun, but it takes work and it must be shared.

What to Do

Timelines are not intended to recall exactly what happened. Rather, they reflect the way history is remembered, and therefore the ways that history continues to influence the present. To create the Basic Timeline of the congregation-in-community, invite a few citizens who share an interest in historical events to join a group of your members who have volunteered (sometimes with encouragement) to recreate the church's story. The invitation to church members to participate in the session should be extended to all who are interested, but be sure to get the input of old-timers who are "soaked" in the church's history. You can use the "Working Notes: Planning for a Basic Timeline" as you plan. You may also want to provide some advance orientation to prompt memories.

On a wall, stretch out a long sheet (perhaps 25 feet) of newsprint or butcher-block paper and enter a few general definitions for units of remembering, such as "Community founding," "Ancient history, pre-1945," "Past generation, 25–40 years ago," "Decades past, 10–25 years ago," "Recent history, past 10 years." Drawing on the collective memory of the group, have a recorder enter on the timeline the significant events, movements, conflicts, and trends that participants say have shaped the

WORKING NOTES:
Planning for a Basic Timeline

Whom shall we invite?

Congregational "old-timers" who really know the history:

Former members from an earlier era:

Members who know recent decades well:

Community residents who have known about the church for a long time:

Background history for advance orientation

What are the key events and dates that should go on the timeline before we start?

community over the years since its founding and the beginning of the church. Pay special attention to the events that occurred during the first years and around the founding, but collapse the decades prior to World War II into fewer sections and allow more space for the years approaching the present.

Divide the paper on which the timeline is drawn with a horizontal line about a third of the way from the top (see Figure 3.1). Above that line, make notes on outside events that have shaped member's lives—national events, such as wars and the Depression; and local experiences, such as population moves, economic development, political struggles, and shared calamities, like fires and floods. On the bottom two thirds of the paper, write notes on the congregation's history. You might anchor your memories with the dates when buildings were purchased or constructed and with the names of pastors and the times of their tenure.

Congregations usually stretch their Basic Timeline back to the church's organizing event, so the committee should be prepared to help the congregation recall (or learn) some basic information on the leaders and circumstances of the early years. The advent and birth of the congregation are important memories to reconstruct for both the community and the congregation, and discussion time should be given in broad strokes to each succeeding era. But allocate your time carefully to allow for discussion of segments of community and congregational history in each division of the Basic Timeline.

Beware: history buffs can be mesmerized by timelines, especially when they want to get it all, and get it right. There is always too much material, and the facts are never exactly right for every observer. Sometimes when the buried bodies of historical fights are uncovered, the committee tries to settle old arguments or they become gun-shy in the face of conflicting viewpoints. You must agree to disagree and then move on, although it may be important later to find ways to address the old secrets and hidden pains that may emerge in this process. When you keep your curiosity high and your expectations modest, your exploration of historical trends can stimulate broad congregational interest, tap a reservoir of

FIGURE 3.1 Basic Timeline

Founding and early days	Ancient history, pre–1945	Past generation, 25–40 years ago	Decades past, 10–20 years ago	Recent history, past 10 years
		Community memories		
Struggling milltown	Town library	Kennedy shot		New immigrant neighbors
	Suburban growth	Main Street mall opened		
	Rock and roll	Vietnam		Computers
		Civil rights	More women in workforce	
Depression	WWII			
		Congregational memories		
Rev. Price (1922–1935)	Rev. Williams (1936–1949)	Rev. Patterson (1950–1972)	Rev. Smith (1973–1976)	Rev. Sherman (1977–1993)	Rev. Doyle (1994–present)
Built church		Mortgage burning			Renovate Sanctuary
		New educational building			Day care
	Mission ties with Burma	Soup kitchen			Praise songs in worship
			First woman pastor		

stories, networks, and hidden connections, and release various streams of unseen energy.

Keep an ear ready for good stories and for commitments that have energized the community and the congregation in the past but are presently dormant. Do they still have the spark of life and could they be rekindled?[3] In particular, enter the dates of crises confronted and resolved, and anniversaries or other celebrations that brought people together. Are the monuments to these events still standing? What events made the community take notice of the church—annual festivals? unfortunate fights?—and when was the congregation affected by community change, such as the advent of rural electrification or the construction of a nearby highway? Note the mysteries of your history—what one congregation called the "untold stories" that have been whispered in the hallways and parking lots but never admitted in "parlor conversation." The Basic Timeline should provide a broad historical foundation for exploring additional aspects of your unique congregational story.

Share Your Work

Leave the timeline posted as a frame of reference for your continuing work. Invite people who missed the development of the timeline to add their stories. Attaching newspaper accounts, especially with photos, will attract additional attention and stimulate sensitivity to the dynamics of change in the community. Ask members to lend the committee artifacts and memorabilia that represent significant community historical events. You may be moved, as one congregation was, to hang the timeline on a wall of the sanctuary to express appreciation for the past and prayerfully seek direction for the future.

Sharing the church's and community's history can be a way of making a long-term investment in your congregation's future. Epworth United Methodist Church, in the Candler Park neighborhood of Atlanta, chose to highlight its history as the gateway to its rebirth. In its building renovation, the first room completed was a "History Room." Collecting pictures, plaques, furniture, and memorabilia into a special room has helped the congregation remember the fun they have had together and the ways people have invested in the church and in one another. Even as they recognized the need to move into the future, they were sure they needed the resources of the past. Those who are now moving into leadership positions at Epworth hope the church's history will not be lost, but used by the members to strengthen their ministry.[4]

Reflection

With this timeline you begin your exploration into the various streams of belief, commitment, family ties, and cultural traditions that have sustained your congregation over the years. You begin the task of helping the congregation not just to remember casually but to think intentionally about both the past and the future. You can guide them into new commitments by collectively remembering the past.

If your exploration identifies major forces and pressures that have shaped both church and community history, it will become easier to understand the decisions of previous generations. When the committee has the empathy to feel the emotions of the past, you may be better prepared to understand the problems you face in the present.

These are theological issues as well: How might you discern the hand of God moving in the community's past? Which of these forces are still strong enough to shape the community's future? With reflection on these questions as background, the committee can look for emerging trends. What new forces and actors are becoming apparent? With the past as prologue, the committee's primary task is to name the forces that are shaping the present, to imagine what may come next for the community, and to ask how God is calling you to respond.

Thinking historically should be a religious practice for the committee. As you accumulate information that "explains" the current situation by setting it in a larger context, you may want to recall, revisit, and perhaps revise the timeline long after you have completed the exercise. In what ways does it help your leadership understand how the events of the present have deep roots in the past? As you look at the shifting landscape of community institutions, can you see more clearly your church's contributions to community welfare in the past, in the present, and possibly in the future?

TIMELINE OF BUILDINGS AND FACILITIES

Background and Rationale

The place where your congregation meets is much more than a utilitarian necessity. It is part of your identity and a key resource (or liability) for your ministry. Assessing the congregation's strengths for the days ahead requires a thorough look at your space—how much you have, what shape it is in, and how it is already used. But spaces have a history, too. Places take on meaning through associations and experiences. You may have heard the lament "If only these walls could talk, what stories they would tell." So let your buildings tell their stories. Take time to explore what has happened in them, what memories remain, and what they mean to the people in your congregation (and perhaps to others in the community).[5]

What to Do

Gather together those who have a primary interest in physical structures and begin creating your *Timeline of Buildings and Facilities* by looking at a large blueprint or wall-sized sketch of the congregation's buildings and grounds. The drawing need not be fancy, but you need a complete "footprint" or overview of your space. Write in the name of each room—

sanctuary or *assembly room, entryway, parlor, classrooms, offices, parking lot, playground,* and the like—in large print so they can be seen from a distance. Use official names, but you get extra points for authenticity if you can add the unofficial "nicknames" they are called by some groups.

Create a written "storyboard" for each significant space. You can use the "Working Notes: Exploring Our Space" to compile this information.

- *Beginnings:* When was this space first acquired? For what purpose? Who wanted it?

- *Use:* What has this space been used for? Who uses it now, for what, and how often?

- *Meaning:* What people or stories are associated with this space? What objects (furniture, symbols, and the like) in it are especially important? What is special or "precious" about it? Name the groups or people who contributed to it.

- *Update:* When was this space last renovated? Who (what group) wanted the renovation? How was it financed?

- *Appearance:* How does this space look? What is its condition and what needs attention?

- *Assets and liabilities:* What does this space "produce," and what has it produced in the past, for members and community groups? Are there any special costs associated with this space? How might it be used in the future?

You may find that the best information is in the closets of the church or even in the homes of present or former church officers, who have cared for the space over the years. Blueprints, pictures, diagrams, even old fundraising programs and annual reports can provide evidence for the changes in the buildings over time. You can dramatize a historical consciousness on the Timeline of Buildings and Facilities by using colors or shaded lines to indicate when buildings were constructed and when they were renovated for new uses.

WORKING NOTES:
Exploring Our Space

My assigned space to explore:

What is its history? (How old is it? Any stories about its beginnings or special events in the past?)

How is it used now?

What makes it special?

What is its current condition, and when was it last renovated?

Assets and liabilities—does it bring in money or cost extra to maintain?

How might you imagine this space being used in the future?

Once you have established basic dates on your storyboard, you can approach a wide variety of people to explore the feelings and meaning that members and people in the community associate with the space. Be sure to identify major donors whose names are associated with particular rooms or objects in the church and record their contributions. Divide the responsibility for studying particular buildings among your committee and visit the assigned spaces while they are in use, if possible. To discover the feelings and meanings associated with various spaces, create conversations with members or community groups who use them frequently, or invite a small group to walk with you through the building. Invite neighbors, members, and even former members to bring in pictures of the building in previous conditions, such as during construction or renovation. Ask them to reminisce about significant events and individuals associated with the space.

Once you have created storyboards for the significant spaces you use, identify key times in history that are relevant to each of them and add those dates to the timeline (see Figure 3.2). Perhaps use yarn to connect stories on the storyboard with points on the timeline. To bring the diagram to life, attach pictures of activities and persons associated with the various spaces. With an imaginative eye, add colorful elements to your Timeline of Buildings and Facilities. Use photographs, colors, and silhouettes to suggest where the most sacred places or special objects are located, where the facility is overused and in need of attention, and how the space might be refurbished for use in the future.

Share Your Work

Post the Building and Facilities Timeline along with the storyboards and other materials from your study where members will have an opportunity to look at it and perhaps add their own comments. The timeline can help them recognize that the uses of the physical resources have changed

FIGURE 3.2 Building Facilities Timeline

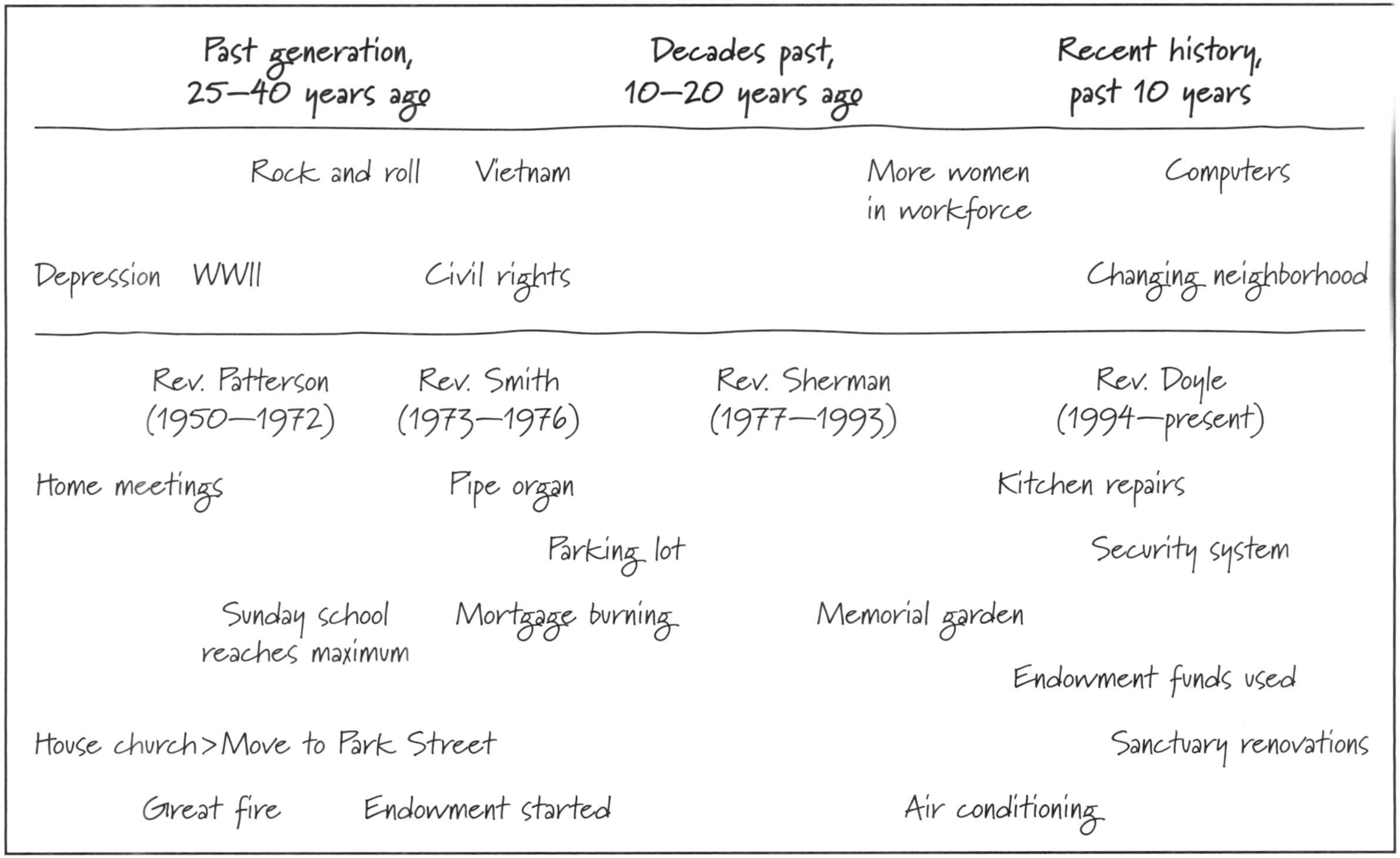

Past generation, 25–40 years ago	Decades past, 10–20 years ago	Recent history, past 10 years
Rock and roll Vietnam	More women in workforce	Computers
Depression WWII Civil rights		Changing neighborhood
Rev. Patterson Rev. Smith (1950–1972) (1973–1976)	Rev. Sherman (1977–1993)	Rev. Doyle (1994–present)
Home meetings Pipe organ		Kitchen repairs
Parking lot		Security system
Sunday school Mortgage burning reaches maximum	Memorial garden	
		Endowment funds used
House church>Move to Park Street		Sanctuary renovations
Great fire Endowment started	Air conditioning	

over time, and accustom them to the possibility of using the space differently in the future.

Reflection

Think about the picture this diagram presents of how your space is presently used (and not used). How have the building and facilities supported your ministry over the years? How have they offered more than you could give or limited what you wanted to offer? Currently, what does your space contribute to who you are and what you do? In this discussion, space has at least two meanings, one physical and the other cultural.[6] Considering the physical realities of your space, how can it contribute to ministries you might undertake in the future? What community needs or potential activities have no home? Conversely, what is being housed in your facility that might be housed better elsewhere?

In terms of its cultural meaning, your space sends a separate message. It can invite people into it or make them feel excluded and unwanted—not by any overt act but just by how it looks. Space always communicates a great deal about the groups that use it. Sometimes what is most precious to one group is a barrier to another. For both physical and cultural reasons, note carefully the similarities and differences between your space and buildings and the other spaces used by the populations and for the activities you reported in your People Map and Institutional Map. How do your architecture and decor differ from what you have seen elsewhere in the community? Is your space a gift of beauty or an eyesore? What do your front door, signs, and parking areas say about how easily a stranger would be welcomed? Would parts of your building be uncomfortable for older or handicapped people? For active children? Although you have made this space your own, who would find it difficult to call this place home?

TIMELINE OF LEADERSHIP AND DECISION MAKING

Background and Rationale

Who gets things done and how do they do it? If you were to ask that question in your congregation, some members might not know and others might be reticent to say what they do know. Because discussions of power and influence can be sensitive, it is best to approach them through a historical review of leadership and decision making in your church. Therefore, this exercise has two phases, study of the past and study of the present. Patterns of past leadership often help to explain how things get done in the present. In this exercise, you will review not only what you did in the past but also *how* you did it. This historical awareness will be especially useful in later role-playing and imagination exercises. In this exercise, you will also see evidence of change—that decisions from the past do not always control the future. Nothing lasts forever.

What to Do

This exercise can be done either by gathering together knowledgeable groups to do the remembering or by undertaking a series of interviews. The information you need will come from people who have been involved in and care about the organizational leadership of the congregation. Some of what you need to know will be found in anniversary histories and committee minutes, but much of it will come from "informed memory." Your first task is to decide who may best remember past eras. Some people were present or remember "what Mama said," and others may be amateur historians.[7] In addition, you will need to identify careful observers of current patterns. Decide whether you will gather a group or groups and who will interview whom.

Historical Patterns   Portraits of former pastors, with hairstyles, clothing, and facial expressions characteristic of their times, often look down from the walls of a church's parlor or entry hall. Beginning with these portraits, or with the pastors listed on your Basic Timeline, identify leaders who seem to have had special impact on the congregation. On a separate sheet for each leader you identify, briefly describe how that person's leadership is remembered. Ask what were considered the person's major accomplishments and how they did it. One pastor might be remembered for a new vision of ministry, another for particularly spiritual sermons, while a third may be associated with pastoral care and a fourth with involvement in justice issues. But how was this leadership exercised? What made this pastor an effective (or ineffective) leader? Were things accomplished because people were inspired by the pastor's sermons, because that person was an exceptional organizer or beloved by all, because lots of financial resources were available, because everyone was swept up in a spiritual renewal? Were there problems because the pastor was weak or domineering or angry? Finally, think about whether these accomplishments have remained part of the church's life. What is this leader's *legacy*? What has lasted and why? You can use the "Working Notes: Remembering Past Leaders" to compile these reflections.

These people did not do it alone, however. Seek to identify the lay leaders who shared in these pastors' struggles and achievements. Seek out stories both about the great men who chaired committees and gave endowments, and about the great women who did those things and perhaps also sustained the church's efforts from behind the scenes. What kinds of people and what kinds of leadership have characterized this congregation at different times in its past? Has a group of "prayer warriors" kept things going through rough times? Have visionary members been willing to risk failure and financial loss to see the church do what it needed to do?

For the various eras in the church's history, accumulate brief descriptions of both pastoral and lay leaders, along with notes about what was

WORKING NOTES:
Remembering Past Leaders

A leader (clergy or laity) who is remembered as important to our church:

When was this person a leader here?

What were this person's most significant accomplishments?

What made this person a good leader?

Was there a down side to this person—things that irritated or alienated people?

What is the legacy of this person's leadership? What has lasted and why?

Can you think of a playful nickname that would describe this leader?

accomplished and how. Where possible, locate pictures and news stories that describe those historical contexts—with church leaders in family settings, in community leadership, and the like. Prepare your notes and pictures for posting at the appropriate places on your Leadership and Decision-Making Timeline. As you did with the other timelines, make this one as colorful and attractive as possible. As you name the unique and sometimes surprising (even shocking) leadership characteristics of former pastors, you may enjoy playfully labeling their portraits, if you have them. (You might use the same playful approach in the role-playing suggested in the next chapter.) Completing this task can make previous leaders seem more real to those who do not remember them.

Contemporary Patterns   Once you have confirmed the diversity of leadership in the past, you will be better prepared to acknowledge the wide differences in patterns of decision making in the present congregation. This portion of the exercise provides a way to visualize the dynamics of decision making by drawing a picture of the flow of information and deliberation as it currently happens in your congregation. A subcommittee may want to undertake this work separately while other members of the team are pursuing the historical patterns.

Pick a recently debated issue—from changing your Sunday morning schedule to hiring a paving contractor for the parking lot. At the top of a sheet of paper, draw a box or circle for the person or organization that first noticed or raised the issue. Then proceed down the page with the steps that were necessary before anything actually happened. Be sure to note the points at which ideas, questions, and decisions were communicated to the congregation as a whole, and how they were communicated. At the bottom of the page, indicate who will be involved in carrying out the action. Official organizations and committees can be represented by boxes on the left, and the unofficial conversations and consultations that help the official process to work can be represented by circles on the right. Figure 3.3 provides an example.

FIGURE 3.3   Decision-Making Diagram

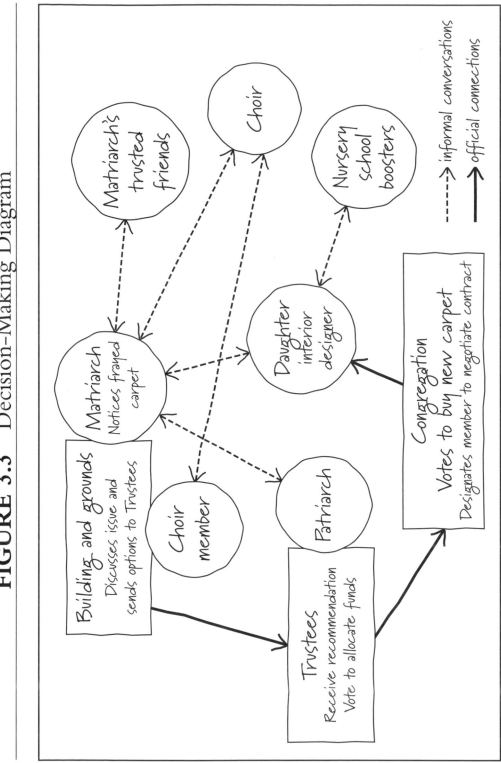

Once you have done one diagram, you may want to develop separate charts for recent decisions and patterns in additional program areas. Make a chart for as many congregational functions as you have time or interest to tackle. Choose the areas that seem most central to what your congregation values about its life together. You will need to develop your own list of issues to track, but we suggest thinking about the following areas of the church's life:

- *Social and fellowship activities.* When the congregation wants to have a social event, who decides what sort of event it will be and makes sure it happens?

- *Welcoming and taking care of members.* When new members join, who makes sure they learn what is expected of them and how to find a place for themselves in the congregation?

- *Taking care of our building.* When something (large or small) needs to get done to the building, who decides what is needed and makes sure it gets done?

- *Providing for children and youth.* When people are concerned about the well-being of the children and youth in the congregation, who worries, organizes, chaperones, teaches, and the like?

- *Community outreach.* When there is a need in the community, who decides what should be done, raises and allocates resources, recruits volunteers, and the like?

- *Meeting spiritual needs.* When there is a need for deepening the spiritual life of the congregation, for making sure that people have the knowledge and spiritual support they need, who tends to the problem?

You can use the "Working Notes: Exploring How We Make Decisions" to plan your exploration.

To develop each diagram, you may need to contact other leaders who have been more directly involved. The point is not to create any sort

WORKING NOTES:
Exploring How We Make Decisions

	A recent decision to explore	Persons to talk with about it
Social and fellowship activities		
Welcoming and taking care of members		
Taking care of our buildings		
Providing for children and youth		
Community outreach		
Meeting spiritual needs		
Other:		
Other:		

of exposé or intrigue. Rather, you want to learn how the congregation moves forward and does its work in a variety of program areas.[8] In some cases, there may be several layers of activity, while in other cases the route from raising an issue to doing something about it may be very direct. Decision making for some programs may occur entirely on the left (official) side of the diagram, while in other decisions most of the activity takes place on the right (informal) side; more often it is a combination of the two. In some cases, the communication is official (which you might represent with solid lines), while other decisions may be characterized by more informal connections (which you might represent with dotted lines). We have seen trustees, for instance, who always make sure they consult with certain trusted and significant contributors, and a missions committee that, as it discusses a new project, consults with a few consistent volunteers to make sure the proposal has grassroots support.

When you have finished your decision-making diagrams, look at all of them together to discern the themes and patterns that characterize the congregation's current leadership. When people look back on this era in twenty or fifty years, what do you think they will see as your legacy? How will they describe how you get things done? Who will they name as the great men and women who make sure the church's ministry happens? Write up a summary to add to the "current times" section of the timeline and include mementos and pictures to symbolize how you work today.

Share Your Work

Select a few leaders and accomplishments from the past to add to the Basic Timeline (along with pictures and whatever else you have collected). Also add some summary phrases describing your current decision-making patterns. Look especially for ties between the struggles and accomplishments of the past and those of the present. These stories may be discussed when you have your final Timeline Celebration.

Having identified particular people who make things happen in primary program areas, you may want to highlight their work in announcements, prayer celebrations, or newsletter articles. Some churches have used the results of their study of decision making to recognize and honor unsung heroes and heroines who work quietly behind the scenes to enable the church to maintain and even expand its ministry.

Reflection

Information gathered in this exercise will be especially helpful in the imaginative, role-playing exercises that follow, and to the accumulated wisdom of the working committee. You should now have a much clearer picture of how and where the energy of the church flows, as well as where the roadblocks may be, as you seek to mobilize the congregation in response to community change. It may be helpful to share some carefully focused material with the congregation, but much of the information you uncover about leadership and decision making will remain in the committee to be used in program implementation.

The working committee may wish to consider some of the lingering questions that emerge as past leadership is compared with present practice:

- Do you see similar patterns in historical and contemporary leaders?

- In what areas does decision making involve a wide range of people, and what decisions are made in a relatively small circle?

- What areas of congregational life are likely to generate lots of social and spiritual energy, personal involvement, and even conflict?

- What is the pastor's role? What areas of work are carried by others, and who are they?

- How are key decision makers related to each other? Along family lines? As old and dear friends? As leaders in key organizations (such as a Sunday school class or choir)?

- What groups are most involved in sharing information and making decisions?

- In what areas are official processes identical with unofficial processes? When are these processes most distinct?

- What is simply not getting done at all?

These questions will require careful and sensitive reflection. Your tentative answers are better used as guidance for the committee itself than as summaries to be posted and shared. In the weeks and months ahead, as you begin to think about planning and implementing changes, these reflections will be a valuable resource.

TIMELINE OF RESOURCES: PEOPLE, MONEY, AND SPIRITUAL PRESENCE

Background and Rationale

Churches are much more than bricks and mortar. They are the people who call them home, along with the gifts and energies these people bring. As the committee reviews these resources, you need to consider the intangibles of the human equation. Individually, members of the congregation bring their personal skills and individual gifts. They also represent networks of connection to other people and resources in the community. Even more, human resources are spiritual as well as physical.[9] The spiritual investment of your members in prayer, personal commitment, and active participation can transform deficits into genuine hope for the future. You will therefore need to take stock in three areas: *money*, *members*, and the unmeasurable but enduring dimension of *spiritual vitality*. By looking at all of these dimensions over time, you will be able to imagine how these resources can be tapped and expanded for the future.

What to Do

This is another set of tasks that you may want to divide up among sub-groups of the committee, or recruit help for from the congregation, for instance, to sort through church records and annual reports to the denomination. Some people enjoy the clarity of keeping good records and can provide you with a historical context to understand better your current situation. "Hard-fact hounds" often gain deep satisfaction from assembling and presenting data in graphic form, showing the patterns of growth and decline over the life span of the congregation.

Chart Your People and Money   Although denominational offices may request membership figures from the official church rolls, we find that average attendance at worship is a more accurate gauge of current member commitment (and a figure that is more easily compared with data from other churches, since definitions of membership differ significantly). You will probably also want to determine membership numbers for relevant periods in your church's history. In addition, record budget figures for the same years. Be aware of anomalies, such as capital campaigns, so you don't end up comparing apples and oranges. Also, if possible, choose an additional measure of participation—church school attendance, for instance—and chart that as well. Having more than one measure of how many people are involved often tells a more interesting story. In the church charted in Figure 3.4, for example, both Sunday school and financial figures in recent years show signs of recovery that are not yet reflected in total membership numbers. As long-inactive older members continue to pass away or move, they are being replaced by new, more active members.

Whatever criteria you choose, gather the appropriate information to produce graphs that suggest the ebb and flow of resources—people and money. Using your Basic Timeline as a guide, choose particular years in which to mark changes over time. Because your goal is to show trends

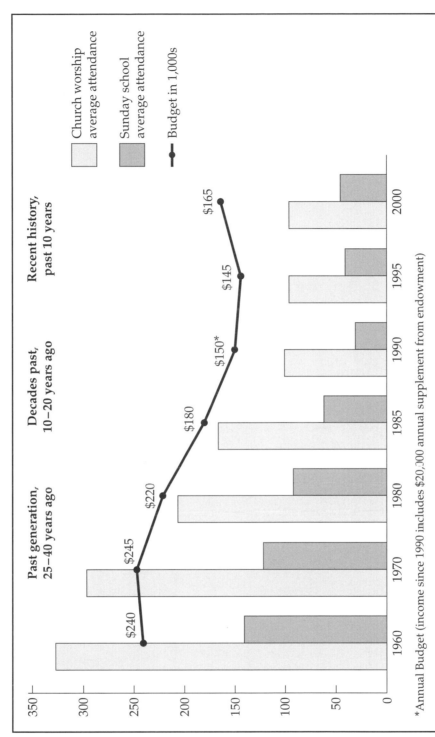

FIGURE 3.4 Resources: Average Attendance at Church Worship and Sunday School and Annual Budget

* Annual Budget (income since 1990 includes $20,000 annual supplement from endowment)

rather than detailed analysis, you can use a single chart to report more than one measure (the number of people and the amount of money, for instance). You can use a combination of bar and line graphs, but be sure to identify each index clearly.[10]

Once your graphs of people and money are complete, begin to explore the implications of this new time chart. What do the lines or bars suggest about the number of members and amount of financial support over the years? When were the times of strong support and when were the seasons of struggle? Look at what you now know about the history of your community: How do your resources reflect the changes in the community as a whole? Do the significant dips or expansions in your budget correspond to major community shifts? Can you see the effects of other factors you have charted in your other timelines?

Chart Your Spiritual Resources   There is another measure that needs to be entered on your time chart, namely, your collective sense of spiritual presence. This is clearly the most subjective judgment we suggest, but the difficulty of making it does not diminish its importance. To develop a measure of spiritual presence, you may want to deploy some of your team to interview members who knew the congregation during the various seasons your timelines have identified as critical periods in the church's history. Individually or in small groups, ask pastors and members how it felt to belong to the congregation during particular periods of strength and struggle. As resources declined, did the sense of spiritual presence also ebb? As the congregation moved through times of crisis, did they feel a resurgence of spiritual presence? How would they describe the presence of the Spirit over time, and how would they sense the Spirit's presence in the current situation?

If a consensus on spiritual presence emerges, create a timeline or bar chart that corresponds to the eras represented on your other graphs and timelines (see Figure 3.5). Congregations frequently report that changes in the sense of spiritual presence precede changes in other areas, for

FIGURE 3.5 Diagram of Spiritual Presence

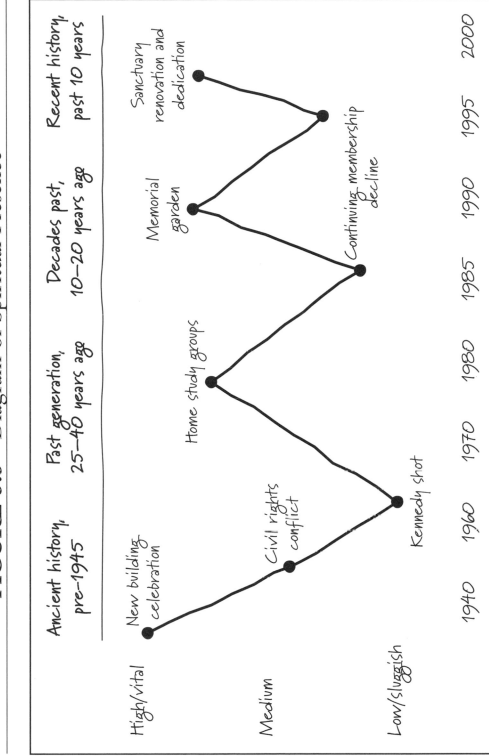

example, it declines prior to membership and financial declines and it shows more strength prior to membership and financial increases. If you are able to discern a pattern, what does it suggest for your congregation?

Share Your Work

As a result of this exercise, you should have two new timelines to share—one that combines average attendance (in worship and church school) with annual financial support, and another that suggests the spiritual vitality of the congregation over time. These two timelines can be posted, perhaps with the spiritual presence measure as an overlay to the financial and membership statistics. They may also be printed in newsletter articles or as bulletin inserts, along with an invitation to discuss their implications. You may want to invite appropriate leaders— such as the chairs of the finance, evangelism, and spiritual nurture committees—to discuss the resource overview. Consider publishing an article in the church's newsletter that highlights the congregation's resources, and include thanksgiving for these gifts in your congregational worship.

Reflection

What do your graphs say about the resources that seem to be available? More important, what have you discovered about your congregation's ability to survive and thrive even when resources seem invisible? What appears impossible may not be so to people of faith. When Moses complained to God that he could not be a leader because he did not have the necessary speaking skills, God had already prepared a creative alternative. Where have you found points of passion and sacrificial giving in the life of your congregation that shed light on the energy you might have for the future? Think—and pray—about how unexpected combinations of resources and faith might make new things possible for you.

TIMELINE OF WORSHIP AND MUSIC

Background and Rationale

Congregations create and use all sorts of practices in their lives together. Not least among these are the particular ways they use symbols, tell stories, and enact the rituals of their faith. Penny Becker's study of congregations illustrates that worship plays different roles in various congregational settings, but for all congregations, worship expresses the central values of their identity.[11] In most congregations, the "service of worship" is the most important event of the week. More people are present than at any other time, announcements of all the congregation's activities are made, and rituals and stories that highlight the congregation's identity and purposes are enacted. We suggest that you use a worship service as a window on the symbols, stories, and rituals that animate your congregation. Look for the activities that make people feel most at home, the symbols that remind them of divine presence, the stories of their own history and of Scripture that they love to tell. These symbols, stories, and rituals can provide strength for survival and courage for new ventures, but they can also be barriers to the integration of new members or ministries. Understanding these key components of your congregation's culture is critical to being able to move ahead in changing times.

Because of worship's foundational significance, church members may believe that their worship form is set in stone, a bedrock identity that never changes, like Jesus Christ, "the same yesterday, today and forever" (Hebrews 13:8). Although permanence may be properly attributed to God, it cannot be said of congregational worship. Every religious group seeks to express its faith through language, artifacts, and actions that best communicate among the participants. Some of these elements, such as Scripture, are very old, and some, such as the language of preaching, are more or less contemporary. This exercise is designed both to give you a more in-depth understanding of your current practices and to place those practices in historical context.

What to Do

Begin this exercise by observing your worship as it exists today, then create a Worship Timeline by naming and locating some of the historical roots that contribute to your worship event. Your observation of worship should involve as many people from your committee as can participate, while your historical research may be delegated to a smaller subgroup.

Observe Today's Worship   One way to look more closely at the meaning of your worship is to deploy your committee as a team of observers, assigning each to watch a particular part of what is happening.[12] You might divide up the task this way:

- *Setting.* Assign one person to look at how the worship space itself is arranged, observing how the room itself directs the action and attention toward one place and away from another, how some areas are highly visible while others are invisible. Pay attention as well to the furniture and special objects that are used. What about lighting and sound? What can you see and hear most easily, and how does that shape your experience of worship?

- *Clothing.* Assign another person to look at the clothing worn by both leaders and participants.

- *Leaders and participants.* Assign a third person to observe who does what. Watch both the official leaders and the ordinary participants. What are the participants expected to do—come in, find a seat, and sit quietly, or be much more vigorously involved? Pay attention to where various people are. Are there spaces that are occupied only by certain persons?

- *Music.* Another person on your team should pay close attention to the music included in the service. What are the styles? Who participates and who leads? How enthusiastic is the participation? Does the music seem to contribute to the worship experience for most of those who are there?

- *Preaching and praying.* Assign one or more persons to listen for what is actually said about and to God. What is the primary story line about what the congregation is doing and should do? Is it about what is wrong with the world? About where hope and strength are to be found? About who God is and what God does in the world? About what God expects of people? What stories (biblical and otherwise) are told? What symbols, words, and metaphors stand out? Is any special jargon used—words and phrases that ordinary people might not understand?

After the committee members have observed a worship service, compare notes and summarize what you have learned. (Each person might prepare for this discussion by using the "Working Notes: Observing Worship.") Create a list of the most important things done in worship and a list of adjectives that would describe the experience of worshiping together. Add this, along with a current order of service, to your Worship Timeline.

Chart the History   Finding out about the history of worship will require the passions of people who are especially interested in music, art, drama, or history, but make sure to recruit people who represent the diversity of worship experiences and preferences in your congregation. As with some of your other work, you may want to establish a subgroup that includes additional people from the congregation. You may also want to enlist the assistance of a reference librarian at your local public (or seminary) library. Some of what you will need can be found in old bulletins and programs, but a few key books on Christian worship can help give even greater historical depth.[13]

Avoid overwhelming the congregation with detail, but concentrate on a few turning points, new beginnings, and significant changes. When (approximate date) did a practice begin, and when did it change into its present form? If you can, locate stories, drawings, pictures, and music from previous generations that can dramatize the changes you identify.

WORKING NOTES:
Observing Worship

My assigned focus is:

Before the service, review suggestions in the chapter for what you should observe, and make notes about what you want to notice:

What I saw (be as detailed and descriptive as possible):

Reflecting on what I saw

What do people seem to care most about?

What would a newcomer find most difficult to understand?

Adjectives that describe what I saw:

Take your historical cues from the key elements you have observed in the current worship service, but among the things you might explore are the following:

- *Scripture.* This is the bedrock of our faith, and its history goes back to the beginning. You probably do not want to start your worship timeline several thousand years B.C., but you may want to note some key eras of scriptural history. When were different portions of the Bible written and canonized? When was it translated into English and what is the date of the translation you now use in worship? Make notes on your Worship Timeline that reflect important changes you discover.

- *Setting.* The gathering place—a sanctuary or auditorium—reflects an early change in Christian history, since the first worship events for Christians were in the homes of members. Consider exploring some of the buildings used by early Christians and see if you can find pictures of church buildings used by your particular denomination early in its history. If your own congregation has had several sanctuaries, find pictures and note how the setting has changed. Add pictures and notes to your Worship Timeline that highlight how things were different in the past.

- *Clergy.* Clearly the first Christians did not employ clergy; only later did they see the need for priests, pastors, and preachers as we know them today. Different faith traditions have made very different decisions about their leadership in general, usually symbolized by their role in worship. Identify leading figures in the formation of your faith tradition and ask your pastor to talk with you about how they are similar to or different from present-day clergy. Has your congregation always had a full-time pastor? Make notes on your Worship Timeline about how your clergy leadership has changed.

- *Clothing.* Particular clothing, such as that worn by clergy, singers, and so on, symbolizes the role of worship leaders. Clearly clothing is different for religious leaders today than it was in the time of Jesus. In your tradition, what clothing is worn by religious leaders and what is its intended meaning? When did your tradition adopt its current commitment to particular clothing for various persons in worship leadership? Make notes and perhaps add pictures to illustrate these changes on your Worship Timeline.

- *Music.* This is the area perhaps most responsive to historical changes and accompanying controversies. Which instruments to use, if any, which singers to include, if any, and what styles of music to use have all been recurring debates in various traditions. When did your church begin using the musical instruments it currently uses, and when were they first introduced into your religious tradition? What sort of music is most often sung by your choir (if you have a choir), and what period or musical tradition does it best represent? About which music is your congregation most enthusiastic, and in what century (or centuries) was it written? On your Worship Timeline, show the roots of your current musical traditions.

- *Participation.* How did congregations in the past behave differently from what you observed today? Have people always sung, read Scripture, and recited unison prayers or creeds, for instance? When did these expectations develop for your religious tradition and for your congregation? Mark on your Worship Timeline when your church adopted its present patterns of participation and when you have seen significant departure from this behavior, such as responses to revivals, emotional funerals, public controversy, and so on.

- *Other.* Every congregation has unique elements (code words, special behaviors) that characterize that particular church as it reflects and interprets the larger tradition. Can you identify your congregation's unique elements? How important are they and when were they added?

You should now have a dynamic picture of how your current worship emerged from many strands of history (see Figure 3.6). You will see its eclectic character, with elements drawn from different centuries woven together to sustain your spiritual journey. The harder task is to explore the continuing effectiveness of your worship, both for your own members and as a bridge of faith to those outside your congregation. This is a more complex task than observing and gathering history. Talk with others in the congregation to supplement what you have learned. Listen for which parts of the service carry the most weight and are most central to the worship experience of your members. How does this differ for nonmembers? What would people miss most if it were gone? Because of the layers of your congregation's particular history, who is most involved and who is marginal to the experience? Which aspects of your worship have the deepest roots in history and which are more current? Which possibly need to be expanded or revised? Two themes should guide your inquiry: How important is each element to the worship experience? and How do various practices detract from worship— for your members but also for those visitors who might join you?

Share Your Work

Post the Worship Timeline next to your other congregational charts and maps. Consider using an adult forum or Sunday school class to share what you have learned about the historical roots of what the congregation does in worship. Ask various members of the congregation to share their experiences and stories of particularly memorable moments. Which elements of worship are most meaningful to them and why? Weave your increased awareness into the worship service itself, explaining and highlighting various practices from week to week.

FIGURE 3.6 Worship Timeline

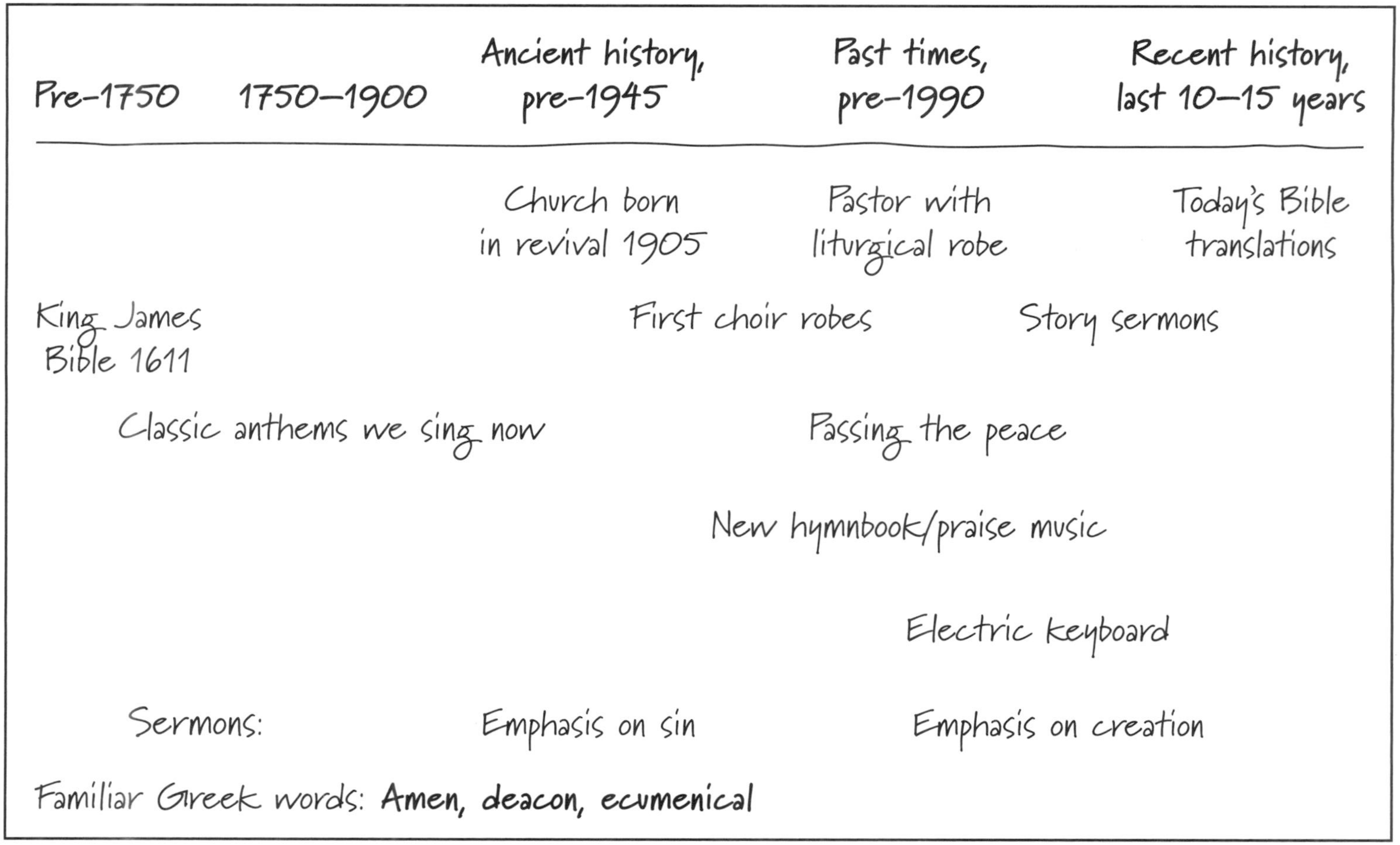

Pre-1750	1750–1900	Ancient history, pre-1945	Past times, pre-1990	Recent history, last 10–15 years
				Today's Bible translations
				Story sermons
		Church born in revival 1905	Pastor with liturgical robe	
		First choir robes	Passing the peace	
			New hymnbook/praise music	
			Electric keyboard	
				Emphasis on creation
King James Bible 1611				
	Classic anthems we sing now			
		Emphasis on sin		
Sermons:				

Familiar Greek words: **Amen, deacon, ecumenical**

Reflection

Getting inside the worship of your congregation is a soul-searching exercise. What sorts of people do you think would find your worship service most meaningful? Who might find it strange or alien? Your reflections on these questions may be helped by visits to nearby churches. Who is there and how are their services different? If you choose to make such visits, consider going with someone you already know in the other congregation, and take the time to learn enough to respect the tradition, so far as is possible, from within.

Think about the things you do and say in worship that make this event most meaningful to your members and most distinctively your congregation's own expression of its relationship with God. Prayerfully list the most important elements. Be sure to include things you always do (spend time passing the peace, for instance) and special events (a Good Friday or anniversary service), along with important symbols (an altar Bible or new choir robes, for instance) and favorite stories (the story of the Exodus, the woman at the well, or your own congregation's founding). Even as these stories and symbols affirm your congregation's experience, how can they be shared with others?

Your timeline should help the congregation celebrate the elements they have chosen to include in their worship. But worship reflects the continual reweaving of ancient truth with contemporary expression, and that implies that the weaving is never done.

SUMMARY CELEBRATION: CREATING A COMPREHENSIVE TIMELINE

Background and Rationale

The information you have accumulated is the raw material for a major congregational event to create a Comprehensive Timeline. This timeline should reflect the congregation's journey and help you imagine where God is leading the congregation in the next chapter of its history. While all of these exercises have required thoughtful expression of the church's story, they have also invited the exercise of spiritual imagination and discernment.

Rather than simply rehearsing problems from the past, creating a comprehensive timeline should be open ended and enjoyable. Participants should have a rare chance to listen to each other's stories and to think together about what they care about most. In addition to what you learn about the congregation in this process, the experience of sharing reinforces the commitment and sense of belonging of those who participate. Embedded in the memories they share and the stories they tell are the themes that hold the congregation together over time.

The potential benefits of such an exercise can be seen in the story of St. Catherine's Catholic parish in Boston. Had they engaged in this sort of comprehensive look at their history and resources, they might have been able to envision a way past their contemporary struggles. They would have noted, for instance, that their worship space, though recently refurbished and large and beautiful, is a striking example of a church designed for pre–Vatican II worship. Personal devotion is encouraged by the shrines and candles and stations of the cross, but there is little sense of communal participation. The leadership of the priest celebrating the Mass in a sanctuary filled with marble and gold trim and high-arched ceilings is awe inspiring but distant. The acoustics are not good and the sound system only works sporadically, so the worshipers can barely hear the priest's words. The music also reflects historical changes—the huge organ that could provide thrilling solo performances is less well-suited to accompanying a congregation in singing. And the congregation, scattered sparsely throughout the room, has little historical awareness of what it must have been like to recite the Creed or the Our Father with hundreds of other worshipers. In addition, a hundred-year-old building poses serious maintenance and repair problems. Ancient wiring and heating systems were installed for a different list of parish programs and the furniture reflects the tastes and styles of a former generation. Not only are their rooms cold and their limited funds exhausted by inefficient systems, but the current members are no longer connected with the warm memories of an earlier age.[14] If the present leaders of the church could engage those who carry the congregation's memories in a candid appraisal of current needs, their collective resources and energy for change might be mobilized.

What to Do

Post your Basic Timeline and add to it the key findings from all your other research. If you have completed each of the previous exercises, select significant items that tell the stories you see as most important in the congregation's history. Make connections with colored yarn and let the artists among you have a field day to dramatize this Comprehensive Timeline. But do not fill up all the space—leave that for the rest of the members of the congregation. If you can, post the other timelines, maps, charts, pictures, and lists as well.

When you are ready, organize an event to celebrate and share your discoveries. Although the Basic Timeline was created by a few invited participants (and others who may have volunteered), push now for maximum participation from members throughout the congregation. Since they have already seen the working maps and timelines on the wall, promise to "tell all, even where the bodies are hid."

Find a space big enough for a major gathering of the congregation. Usually this event is scheduled for an evening with a potluck or covered-dish dinner. The sharing of food is certainly an appropriate setting for sharing memories of the past and hopes for years to come. Typically, churches advertise this event as "A Night to Remember" or "Sharing the Story."

Begin with a review of the committee's experience in gathering the information and share the highlights of your activities. At this point, many congregations engage their members by inviting everyone to write their initials on the Comprehensive Timeline at a point corresponding to the time of their earliest memories of the church. Then encourage participants to tell stories about what the congregation was like at various points in its history. Have a recorder make brief notes on the timeline, summarizing the key events and the descriptions your participants offer. Encourage members to add their memories of personal events (such as weddings and baptisms), celebration events (such as the way Christmas used to be), and broad activities in education, outreach, and church life.

Among the sorts of things you may want to prompt members to remember about each era in the congregation's history are the following:

- What are your earliest memories and feelings about the congregation?

- What traditions or activities were your favorites and why?

- What sorts of people (and how many) were part of the church then?

- What sorts of programs did the church have then?

- How did people help each other?

- What were the high points and low points, the great accomplishments and the most difficult struggles?

- What was the congregation's reason for existing, its mission? What did everyone want to make sure the congregation provided for its members and for the community?

In the second phase of this exercise, invite participants to identify the themes that have sustained your congregation throughout its history. On a separate sheet of newsprint, list the values and commitments that have always been important to the congregation (see Figure 3.7), such as the following:

FIGURE 3.7   Reflections on a Timeline: Themes That Have Sustained Us

- Caring families
- Excellent preaching and worship
- Rich musical tradition
- Strong lay leaders
- Bible study groups
- Good friends over the years

- What have been the key mission emphases, the central goals of the congregation?[15]

- Is this a church that exists primarily to provide a spiritual refuge for its members? Or is it a place that wants to change the world?

- Does this church want to be of service to the larger community, a gathering place in times of crisis and celebration?

- Is it intent on bringing as many people to faith as possible?

- Is it primarily a place where families raise their children? Or is it a place where outcasts from the community find a home?

The answer to any or all of these questions may be yes, but you will be helped if you encourage those who have spent time telling the congregation's stories to take a step back and say something about what they think it means.

Finally, considering both your history and your values, what might be the next chapters in your congregational history? How do you think the story will continue to unfold? What traditions are likely to be left behind? How might an old theme be resurrected for a new time? Reserve at least fifteen minutes at the end of the allotted time to look back at what you have learned. Are there distinct chapters in the history you have created? If so, label them in different colors on the timeline. Each chapter title might even be a metaphor or a mythical or biblical reference (Genesis, Garden of Eden, Golden Era, Testing, Phoenix, and such). What chapter titles might reflect your congregation's story? And most important, what is the next chapter? Where do you go from here?

This event usually ends with praise, song, and prayer—and often a round of spontaneous testifying (even in reserved congregations) about "what this church means to me."

SUMMARIZING YOUR WORK

It is now time to provide a grand overview of the panoramic view you have created of the congregation's life. In preparation, each group member might respond to the questions on the "Working Notes: Reflecting on Our History." In addition to the Comprehensive Timeline, you might now construct a series of lists, such as "What we do well," "Our favorite stories," or "We've always done it this way." A list with this last title might allow your congregation to take a critical (or even comical) look at its sacred cows. Congregations that undergo significant change must challenge their assumptions about how things get done. If you have already learned to recognize (and laugh about) the ways in which you are stuck in the mud, you will be miles ahead in the process of getting yourselves out of ruts in which you do not want to stay. Post your lists or report them at a congregational gathering, inviting discussion of what you have found. These summary impressions will lay the foundation for the next steps on your journey.

WORKING NOTES:
Reflecting on Our History

If someone asked me about our church, I'd tell them this story:

I'm proud that our church has . . .

We are *so predictable* when we . . .

I was surprised to learn that *we haven't always* . . .

What "tender spots" in your history may still need healing?

What usable gifts has your past given you for the future?

Suggestions for Further Reading

1. The process developed by Future Search is most widely used by commercial and community groups but less known among congregations. See Marvin R. Weisbord and Sandra Janoff, *Future Search: An Action Guide to Finding Common Ground in Organizations and Communities* (San Francisco: Berrett-Koehler, 1995). An overview of several major approaches can be found in Barbara Benedict Bunker and Billie T. Alban, *Large Group Interventions: Engaging the Whole System for Rapid Change* (San Francisco: Jossey-Bass, 1997).

2. For an extended discussion and graphic examples of developing timelines that emphasize either the congregation or the community, see *Studying Congregations*, pp. 43–45 and 209–210.

3. Herbert Anderson and Edward Foley, in *Mighty Stories, Dangerous Rituals: Weaving Together the Human and the Divine* (San Francisco: Jossey-Bass, 1998), show how these stories can be sustaining sources for families and congregations. Gary Gunderson, in *Deeply Woven Roots: Improving the Quality of Life in Your Community* (Minneapolis: Fortress Press, 1998), also shows how stories have the power to preserve and transform communities.

4. See Ammerman's *Congregation and Community*, p. 277.

5. Additional suggestions for understanding the significance of space can be found in *Studying Congregations*, pp. 91–92.

6. A greatly expanded discussion on the meaning of sacred spaces in congregational life can be found in *Studying Congregations*, pp. 156–164.

7. For an excellent introduction to exploring congregational histories (including an assessment of the sometimes limited usefulness of anniversary publications), see James P. Wind, *Places of Worship: Exploring Their History* (Nashville, Tenn.: American Association for State and Local History, 1990).

8. Several different approaches to the formal and informal dynamics of congregational leadership can be found in the chapter on process

in *Studying Congregations,* especially the discussion beginning on p. 107.

9. An additional discussion of the wide-ranging resources among members can be found in *Studying Congregations,* pp. 134–135.

10. Those who want to expand on this brief discussion will find extensive guidance and examples of ways to present budget materials in the chapter on resources in *Studying Congregations,* pp. 142–156.

11. *Congregations in Conflict: Cultural Models of Local Religious Life* (New York: Cambridge University Press, 1999), by Penny Edgell Becker, explores four typical models of how congregations do things together. Some churches are primarily *houses of worship,* some are *families,* some are *communities* in which members deliberate and express their individual values, and some seek to be *leaders* in their religious traditions and in community contexts. You may benefit from comparing your own congregation's culture to those she describes.

12. An excellent guide to observing congregational worship and culture can be found in *Studying Congregations,* pp. 199–202.

13. Extensive resources are available for those interested in the history of Christian worship practices. Some of the best and most accessible include Paul F. Bradshaw and Lawrence A. Hoffman, eds., *The Making of Jewish and Christian Worship* (Notre Dame, Ind.: University of Notre Dame Press, 1991); William H. Willimon, *Word, Water, Wine, and Bread: How Worship Has Changed over the Years* (Valley Forge, Pa.: Judson Press, 1980); and James F. White, *Christian Worship in Transition* (Collegeville, Minn.: Liturgical Press, 1997).

14. For more on this case, see *Congregation and Community,* p. 69.

15. In the book *Varieties of Religious Presence* (New York: Pilgrim Press, 1984), David Roozen, William McKinney, and Jackson Carroll describe different "mission orientations" and introduce readers to various congregations that embody these contrasting strategies. You might find these points of comparison useful as you think about your own central values.

CHAPTER FOUR

LOOKING FOR PILLARS OF FIRE

While the Israelites were slaves in Egypt, God invited them to imagine an alternative—"a good and broad land, a land flowing with milk and honey." By this point in your journey, you have gathered significant information on social maps and timelines about your congregation and those who share your terrain. You have noticed many relationships between the community and the congregation, some positive and intimate, some distant and difficult. Now you need to make sense of what you have discovered, but the task is much more than a rational analysis. Like the Israelites in Egypt, you need to imagine the new relationships to which God is calling your church. As you begin this envisioning process, remember that imagining alternatives is not easy. Even though they were slaves, the Israelites grumbled at the thought of leaving their wellworn ways. It is always painful to abandon comfortable old realities (or illusions) to risk new and unproven possibilities. These exercises are designed to expand your perspectives and stimulate your willingness to risk.

Courageous congregations that open their eyes to the world around them are likely to discover that they are not in familiar and predictable

109

"Egypt" anymore. Engaging in adaptive change can feel chaotic when all the usual landmarks have disappeared. Like living in the biblical wilderness, when you discover that the local economy is not what you knew, even when it involved making bricks without straw, difficult questions arise. What sorts of new skills might you have to learn? When the local cuisine does not include "fleshpots and bread," what sorts of "manna" will you be able to discover in your new landscape? Will you, like the Israelites, be willing to live day by day in the difficult and sometimes extended years of transition, with only the vision of milk and honey to sustain you?

The purpose of this chapter is to enact the feelings and intone the voices of an envisioned future. In these exercises, you are asked to play roles, act out viewpoints, and speak from various perspectives that generally are not yet your own. In our experience, describing a situation is not the same as being there, and explaining a transition is not the same as making the change—even in playacting. Not all congregational committees with whom we have worked have accepted our invitation to attempt this method of imagination, preferring a more rational approach of discussing and weighing options and making strategic plans. But those who have taken the risk have reported that each exercise repaid their effort with new energy—but only when they threw themselves into the activity with what they called "reckless abandon."

The first set of exercises, the Wilderness Exercises, invites you to try on five different paths toward the future and in the end to seek the particular "pillar of fire" that will guide you forward. Having discerned your way forward, you will return to imagining how your vision might become reality. The Imagination Exercises will take you back into all the data you have gathered but will ask you to imaginatively experience the connections that might exist between who you now are and who you might become. What would it really be like to live on the other side of the Jordan?

If you have not already incorporated prayer into the regular routine of your working group, now is the time to do so, and to invite your congregation to support you with prayer as well. The process of spiritual discernment is so crucial at this phase that you will find the reflection sections before the "Share Your Work" sections in this chapter. They are simply integral to the work you are doing. Although we offer you practical exercises for envisioning your changing ministry, remember that it is ultimately God whose vision you seek.

ENCOUNTERING THE WILDERNESS

Most congregations faced with changes in the community to which they minister are tempted to tinker, and sometimes tinkering is enough. But tinkering does not lead to transformation. Congregations that undergo deep changes find the strength and imagination for those changes only when they have faced all the possibilities—including death.[1] Only when they feel the dark, tangled uncertainty of transitional moments do they develop the faith resources essential for their transformation. Only when congregations can really imagine letting everything go can a new life be born in them. But facing these possibilities is frightening and risky. It is venturing into a wilderness that takes us far from the safety and predictability of home.

When we find ourselves in such an uncertain and seemingly helpless state, we should remember that God is not absent. When the Israelites found themselves a long way from home, the Exodus story tells us, "they looked towards the wilderness and the glory of the Lord appeared" (Exodus 16:10). Note that they did not look back toward Egypt to see God; rather, they turned to face the wilderness. In this time of decision, as you face the wilderness of change, you will need to be especially attuned to God's presence out ahead of you. Therefore, we offer this set of Wilderness Exercises that are intentionally disruptive to name the possible paths that lie ahead and release the congregation for intentional, constructive decisions.

These exercises will plunge your working group into the wilderness with a series of activities designed to dramatize the situation and imagine the options, along the way exploring the potential risks and gains that might result from engaging new forms or emphases in your ministry.[2]

Creative ministry begins more with energy than with analysis, more with passion than with rational priorities. Discerning commitment is a wilderness experience, an art form, not a science. To explore commitment, you will need to find ways to translate feelings into whispers and to amplify those whispers into voices that can be heard in the discussions where decisions are made.

The process begins with *Testing Your Choices*, in which your study committee will be challenged to say out loud and explore fully the most unthinkable options and the most extreme choices. In *Discerning the Directions*, you will share the intentional drama of choice in a larger forum, seeking to engage the energy of faith-based commitment. This dramatic experience should include a broad network of key figures and interested others from both the congregation and the community. In *Naming the Pillar of Fire*, you will translate these experiences into well-aimed words that embody your emerging vision. Finally, in *Imagining Life Across the Jordan*, you will anticipate conversations that might occur when you put your decisions into action. Although each of these exercises can be completed in a single meeting, for maximum impact you are strongly advised to spread them out, perhaps meeting weekly, with additional time on retreat, until the task is completed. A minimum of two months is usually necessary to explore all the alternatives and work through the feelings they arouse.

The opportunity to imagine can be creative, playful, and exhilarating. Remember to enjoy the process, to laugh and weep, to expose the extremes so that your ultimate decisions may be anchored in full disclosure and bedrock faith.

WILDERNESS EXERCISE 1: TESTING YOUR CHOICES

Background and Rationale

Everyone's normal reaction to the notion of change is to think about "doing things differently." Much of this workbook is aimed at exactly that. However, sometimes change is not doing things differently but about imagining different outcomes. In this exercise, we expose and explore the most foundational decisions facing congregations.

In studying a variety of changing communities, Ammerman discovered that change consistently comes in a few basic models—with as many variations on the themes as there are congregations[3]:

1. Some congregations choose to continue as they are, without changing. Many of these will slowly die, but a few choose to bring their ministry to a deliberate close and intentionally distribute their assets to others who can carry on in new ways.

2. Other congregations move out of the old location and into a new one.

3. As new populations seek places of worship, many new congregations are formed, some of them "sheltered" by existing ones.

4. Other churches redefine their place in the old community by finding a new niche, a recognizable ministry that allows them to reach beyond a single neighborhood.

5. A few congregations "reroot" themselves in the old location by welcoming new members, beginning new ministries, and transforming their old ways of doing things.

A sixth model is really a combination of all the others. Some congregations choose to merge with another existing congregation, pooling their resources for a fresh start. While this is a distinct way to respond, the challenges of merger encompass the challenges of pursuing the other paths. For example, congregations that merge have to recognize that in some sense the old congregation is gone. They face grieving and stewardship tasks similar to those of dying churches. In another sense, merged congregations face all the uncertainty and liability of being new. If they move, they add those challenges to the mix. If they seek to reroot or find a niche, the work will be no less difficult than if they were doing it in their former guise. Indeed, merged congregations multiply the challenges. If you are considering merger, simply be aware that you will be choosing a combination of the paths you will explore in this exercise.

Note that each of the five primary options implies different definitions of *community* and different ways of relating to that community. In this multipart exercise, you are asked to try on each of those ways of changing. In each section, you will ask the hard questions, discussing each option as if it were the only alternative and listing the assets and liabilities of that option. (The "Working Notes: Imagining the Options" can help participants prepare for this discussion.) You may want to explore all five options in one meeting or divide them up for discussion during more than one session. If your group is large enough, you may wish to divide into subgroups, with each discussing only one of the options.

The effectiveness of this exercise depends on the stark drama of difficult choices and emotional commitments.[4] Everyone participating needs to explore each option as if it were the only choice.

Participation You may want to enlarge your working group to include other congregational leaders as well as community participants from outside the circle of congregational membership. Be sure to include a representative group. The work will also need skilled and caring leadership, so you may want to bring in a neutral outside consultant or a denominational staff member to help you engage each option more fully. Congregations are usually reluctant to engage in divisive discussion, but we believe they can gain by "confronting the giants" directly rather than in dissident, whispered discussions in the hallways and parking lots.[5] As we noted at the very beginning of this workbook, creative engagement of conflict is one of the hallmarks of congregations that change successfully.

Recording Someone should take responsibility for recording the primary ideas and arguments for each option. This is best done on large newsprint so that the participants can see the record as it is being written and make their additions and suggestions accordingly. The scribe should keep a record of the major content themes rather than every detail. If possible, the scribe should also note the significant feelings, even passions, that

WORKING NOTES:
Imagining the Options

From the five primary options for the future, I'm preparing to argue for
_____ as if it were the only option.

Background or past experiences I can draw on:

Arguments I will advance for this choice:

Information I should find to support my arguments:

Biblical or faith resources I can use:

Commitments and feelings of others I will solicit:

For personal reflection only:
Emotional commitments I anticipate in myself:

Results I hope for from this discussion:

are expressed about these themes. This record will be important as preparation for the second Wilderness Exercise.

What to Do

Option 1: Death   No human institution is meant to last forever; to claim otherwise would be to claim for our own creation something that belongs only to God. For some congregations that have lost touch with a meaningful community in which to minister, the end seems only a matter of time—perhaps a few years, perhaps less. A responsible and discerning congregation should be honored for making a decision to end their story and to take seriously the bequeathing of their worldly goods to other congregations that can carry on the ministry. Even with high commitment among a declining number of aging members, many persistent urban congregations do not survive.

Try It On. At an appointed time when you are fully prepared, consider as honestly as you can the option of closing the church permanently. Discuss the simple trajectory of existing data: If you do not change, what is the future of your congregation? If the congregation died, what would be missing in the world? Would the dispersal of your resources be a net gain or a net loss? Do you have a faith language to explain this to the congregation, and how would they respond? Put both facts and feelings into your notes, argue as strongly as possible, make the case as realistic as possible, and save your newsprint for the next exercise.

Option 2: Moving   Moving to a new neighborhood and a new or different facility is often seen as a cop-out. Some would claim that congregations that move have failed to face the realities of the urban world and are unwilling to make the necessary changes. At the same time, simple honesty dictates that some congregations may evaluate their current resources and find them totally unsuited for new ministries in their current location. If you began this journey assuming that your neighborhood would be your community, you may have discovered that other religious groups are effectively serving the neighborhood and are looking for just the sort of home your building might offer. Or you may have surveyed an aging building and concluded that it is not useable for anyone's future. It may even be that changing patterns of land use in the neighborhood make it an inhospitable place for the sort of worship and ministry your congregation envisions.

Moving to a new location, then, may be a component in the overall vision that emerges for your congregation. Being good stewards of what you leave behind and taking into full consideration the needs that remain are essential parts of the task. Much of the work of adaptation will still be required, even if the programs and constituents of the congregation remain the same. To leave behind old space will require mourning, and to make new space functional will require adaptive work. In the process, new members are likely to arrive and old ones to leave.

Try It On. If you were to move, what would it cost and what might you gain? If you were to move, what would you take along? Who would you want to become? In the language of faith that your congregation would understand, how would you describe moving as mission and ministry? Who in the church would be convinced and who would not? Why? Make a newsprint list of the issues discussed and the feelings expressed as preparation for the next exercise.

Option 3: Birthing a New Congregation   In the long run, most of the change in how ministry gets done takes place through the creation of whole new congregations. New congregations often have the ability to concentrate energy on the most immediate current needs, speaking the language (often literally) of those who might find existing congregations alien. Since they do not have to spend energy revamping old structures, there is more energy for creating new ones.

New congregations, however, are fragile. Until they reach a size sufficient to sustain themselves, they are at risk in ways that older ones are not, because they have no reserves of experience, resources, and reputation on which to draw. New congregations are often helped in all three of these areas by the sponsorship of a denominational organization that can provide wisdom, money, and a recognized identity. They may also be helped by being adopted by an existing congregation that offers not only a place to meet but other forms of support and recognition as well.

Try It On. Look honestly at the need to initiate new congregations to reach emerging population groups. What sorts of new congregations would be welcome and needed in your community? What sorts might face opposition? Should your congregation help to sponsor a new congregation? What would it be like to be in partnership with a group that is significantly different from you? How would you explain this, in faith, to your congregation? Record the themes of your conversation in preparation for the next exercise.

Option 4: Finding a Niche   As urban regions become increasingly criss-crossed by associations that go beyond geography, so congregations are increasingly defined by those same dispersed associations. Some congregations clearly continue to be identified by the particular place where they are located, but most are identified by some combination of geographical and cultural categories—where they are and who they serve. Some are associated with a given neighborhood and at the same time known as the "Bible-believing," "family-oriented," "mission-minded" church or as the "high church with great music" and "that place with the exciting social ministries."

Not every person who seeks out a congregation needs to work and worship in exactly the same way, and not every congregation in a given area needs to serve every need of that community. There is room for variety in the many ways faith communities are gathered. Discerning God's call to a special ministry that few others would be able to provide is no less honorable than hearing a call to minister to and with one's immediate neighbors. You may already have envisioned a potential niche as you defined your community boundaries—drawing a wide geographical circle but focusing on a particular part of the population and a particular set of institutions within that circle.

Finding a niche may not call for a great deal of internal change in a congregation. Rather, it may call for enhancing what is already done well and enlarging the networks of communication that can get the word out to the particular groups that will find your ministry most meaningful. It will demand focused energy and a willingness to let go of parts of the past in order to facilitate the emerging ministry.

Try It On. Begin with a list of possible niche ministries that could make sense for your congregation. From what you know of the congregation and the community (however broadly defined), what are your several options? Then concentrate on the most likely option. If you focused on a particular niche, what niche would it be and what would you need to do to be the kind of congregation needed by that group of people? What would probably be sacrificed and what would be expanded? How does such a niche fit into your congregational faith as it is now expressed and practiced? How might that faith be affected by selecting such a niche? Prepare your record for the next exercise, highlighting the brightest prospects and recognizing the potential losses.

Option 5: Rerooting in the Old Neighborhood   This is perhaps the most difficult of the options. Of the congregations Ammerman surveyed in nine rapidly changing neighborhoods, only about 15 percent undertook this sort of transformation. It involves new forms of outreach, welcoming new members, learning new cultural patterns, and finding new ways to make decisions. If you set your community boundaries close to your current neighborhood, you have been surveying the diverse populations that surround you and getting to know the needs and resources in the area. It is now time to ask whether you are ready to leave your old identity behind to work with these new neighbors to create a new chapter in your congregation's story.

Try It On. Are there significant new populations in your neighborhood with whom you can imagine being in ministry? Do you have the necessary resources to survive a period of transition? Are you really ready to give up old ways of doing things? Record the highlights of your conversation for use in the next exercise.

Summary Exercise: Merging Your Congregation with Another

Because church merger is often the combination of all five options, as noted earlier, it is the most complex and challenging alternative confronting the congregation. For that reason, you may use the prospect of church merger to review the arguments and emotions you have experienced in the discussion of each separate option. For example, as in choosing *death*, your old congregation will disappear—your name will be changed, the taken-for-granted quality that made membership so comfortable will disappear, and like the Israelites in the wilderness, some of your members will wish you had simply died. As in the option of *moving*, in merger you may actually relocate to work and worship in another place; or if you remain and the other congregation comes to your building, at minimum some of their "sacred furniture" will be imposed into your space. As in *birthing a new congregation*, in merger a body of new members will come among you, bringing new resources (for which you will be grateful) but also bringing their own leaders and member expectations and trampling unaware upon your established ways of doing things. As in *finding a niche*, in merger you may recognize that your members are no longer neighbors but scattered throughout the region, stretching your resources to maintain clear communication, a strong sense of community, and significant commitment among your members. As in *rerooting in the old neighborhood*, in merger you must find ways to bridge your differences and mix several cultural streams into a single, unified congregation, seeking common ground while maintaining separate histories.

Try It On. Let all the options speak at once, in one brief cacophony of advocating voices. This chaotic exercise should last only a few minutes and should provide some much-needed comic relief to the serious questions raised previously. At the same time, it will immediately explain why the managerial mathematics of mergers ($1 + 1 = 2.5$) is so different from the common experience (namely, $1 + 1 = 0.5$). First, enjoy the dissonance with deep appreciation for the life-long investment of emotions these sounds reflect. Then take significant time to explore the possible gains of a merger that survived the transition. What would worship look like? What leadership would emerge? What ministries might evolve? Record these deliberations and prepare for the next exercise.

Reflection

The power of this series of deliberations lies in the focus on each option "as if" it were the most persuasive—to drink from the dregs of a cup that you may ultimately reject. If you let yourselves, this can be a powerful and revealing exercise, a reflection of the congregational wilderness in slow motion. As you explored each option, where did you begin to catch a glimpse of the vision and energy you will need for the future?

Share Your Work

You are probably not yet ready for extensive public sharing of this exercise. The larger congregation and community will be brought into this process later, as you will see.

WILDERNESS EXERCISE 2: DISCERNING DIRECTIONS

Background and Rationale

After you have looked bravely at this range of possible futures, it is time to lay them out together and make a commitment. Although you may have expressed both feelings and facts as you explored each of the options, discussing them separately may have become far too analytical and rational. By undertaking a mock political debate, recapping what you learned in the previous exercise, the committee and an enlarged circle of participants can seek the particular path you are called to follow.

Allow some time after you have completed the first Wilderness Exercise for the discussion to sink in. Make sure that others in the congregation understand the process you are undertaking. Knowing that you have seriously explored the idea of moving or closing your doors may precipitate a good deal of worry or anger if the congregation does not understand the "as if" nature of your discussions. Invite key leaders in the congregation into the discussion, and consider the best format and audience for this next exercise. Because you are moving toward important decisions about your future, the participants in this exercise should include key stakeholders. Because imagining radical new directions can be emotionally wrenching, some committees have chosen to limit the participants to the working committee and their guests, and to report on the proceedings to the rest of the congregation later. We believe, however, that this exercise could be undertaken by a whole congregation, perhaps in a retreat setting, possibly even in morning worship. Such a congregation-wide exercise needs the guidance of a skilled professional leader, but including the entire congregation could help unify energy for transition.[6]

What to Do

Post as props all of the lists you produced as you struggled with each option for the future (facing death, moving, midwifing a new congregation, finding a niche, rerooting in your old neighborhood). Select a moderator and a spokesperson for each of the options. Use your notes from the previous exercise as resources, but add additional information and feelings that have arisen since your lists were first prepared. Each spokesperson should take about five minutes to summarize the arguments for that option, arguing as persuasively as possible, as if it were the best possible option.

As you conclude the "as if" presentation, open the conversation to engage everyone assembled in a lively discussion about what you have all heard and experienced. This is an imaginative excursion into the wilderness, with participants willing to express their feelings as they consider options of death and new life. It is an opportunity for negotiation, for exploring any combination of mix-and-match options, such as death of the present church but birth of a new one, merger with another church to launch a niche congregation of a particular sort, or having another congregation move in with yours and together rerooting the ministry among the new residents of your changing community.

Note on "staging" this exercise: Everyone needs to be reminded of the "as if" character of the opening arguments and the opportunity for responses after the initial presentations. If the positions are presented forcefully, this Wilderness Exercise can be highly emotional and easily misunderstood. All participants should understand that the presentations are intentionally strong and passionate so that everyone can listen carefully for the moments when God's Spirit may break through.

After the initial exchange and conversation, allow time for prayerful reflection. Begin by asking each participant, both audience and presenters, to spend five to fifteen minutes alone—don't rush it. As they reflect on the experience, they should quietly make notes in at least two areas:

- In what direction do you feel your congregation is being called?
- How would you describe the faith and the feelings that surround that choice for you?

The "Working Notes: Reflecting on the Options" may be useful as you collect these thoughts and feelings.

After this time of solitary reflection, have everyone return to the gathered group, share notes, and seek to find a common path through the wilderness. This is not a vote in which the majority "wins," but a time of mutual respect when together you seek to hear the voice of God speaking to you. Reaching the "mind of the church" may take more than a single meeting, but once it is discerned, it should release great energy of deep conviction.

WORKING NOTES:
Reflecting on the Options

What arguments do you recall as most persuasive from each of the five (or more) choices that were role-played?

Death:

Moving:

Birthing a new congregation:

Finding a niche:

Rerooting in the old neighborhood:

Merging:

Other (specify):

Put a check by one or several choices that represent the ways you feel God is calling your church.

What information and arguments support your sense that this is God's call?

What faith commitments and feelings support your sense that this is God's call?

Prepare a brief (one-line) prayer for discerning God's will to share with your committee when you gather.

Notes about unpacking the experience: As you think back, what are your personal feelings after participating in the role-playing exercise? Did you say all you intended? Were you fair with others? Were they fair with you? Is there anything you need to say "out of role" to clear the air and complete the exercise?

Reflection

Beyond the immediate decision, this experience can provide a time of sustaining spiritual strength. What did you discover about your church (and yourselves) in this experience? Is it worth keeping the congregation together? In this place or in a new one? Can you celebrate your past without getting caught in crippling nostalgic memories and idolatry of your sacred places? Can you imagine being satisfied with Christian worship in another language or a different cultural format? Does this experience sharpen or shatter your faith? Why? As you name commitments and resources that are becoming essential for ministry at this time, like the Israelites you must also recognize the need to give up the comfortable old ways. What is God showing you that you can leave behind in Egypt? What is precious as a foundation for the future and what are you willing to sacrifice for that future?[7]

Share Your Work

Remember that those who have not been down all the wilderness roads with you need now to share the struggles, the catharsis, and the emerging vision. If you did not involve the whole congregation in the exercise itself, you will need to find ways to share with them the vision of the future that has come out of weighing these options. A worship service or congregational meeting, as well as newsletters and informal conversations, can be critical at this point.

WILDERNESS EXERCISE 3: NAMING THE PILLAR OF FIRE

Background and Rationale

For the Israelites, the way forward was marked not by a path or map but by their willingness to follow the cloud by day and the pillar of fire by night. Now that you have spent time discerning your direction of change, it is time to name that direction in a way that will make it memorable. It is time to put together what you are now imagining into an initial Vision Statement that will guide your work in the coming months, perhaps years. For our purposes, the Vision Statement is not a comprehensive expression of all that you believe, nor is it a strategic plan for specific ministries. Rather, your Vision Statement should distill many planning disciplines into a succinct, authentic, and functional few words that link the strength of your past with the best hopes for your future. To write a Vision Statement, church leaders have adapted procedures from many sources—from biblical prophets to corporate boardrooms, from spiritual retreats to political battles. Whatever procedures are used, the Vision Statement should be clear, compelling, and flexible, drawing on your imagination as much as your planning skills.[8]

For example, First Presbyterian Church in Hartford, Connecticut, summarized their churchwide conversations in a single sentence: "A richly diverse Hartford congregation building a warm and caring community that spiritually nurtures people in worship, education, fellowship, and active involvement in mission." When it came time for an ad in the local paper, they cut even closer to the bone: "An inviting church drawing diverse people together in worship and service." Finally, when they developed large banners to affirm their commitment to the community, they reduced their Vision Statement to a sketch of the building and four words in bold print and hung the banners from the steeple and lampposts on the street: "Welcoming, Including, Enlightening, Encouraging." A Vision Statement, then, simply provides a way to concentrate the faith-energy of the congregation in a new or renewed direction.

What to Do

The working group needs to define the congregation's Pillar of Fire in a simple, brief statement based on what you have discovered in these Wilderness Exercises. This Vision Statement should express in one or two sentences (twenty-five to forty words) the direction and hope toward which you feel called at this time as a people of God. As one church leader urged, "Let's write poetry, not bylaws!" Collectively, the working group should search for language that expresses the urgency of God's spirit moving in and through the congregation.[9]

Reflection

This exercise provides a time for soul searching, a moment of truth when you are challenged to name the focal point of energy and commitment for the next phase of your congregational ministry and mission. Is your statement specific enough for action, yet sufficiently broad to be creatively applied? Are you outside the box enough to reach elements of the changing community, yet sufficiently within the faith tradition to gain membership support? Are you really listening to the voices of the congregation and community, and in all of them hearing the voice of God?

Share Your Work

The results of this exercise will depend on how well your working group is able to help others in the congregation to own the statement you have devised. Such ownership will be the product of many conversations—in public and private—among the planning committee, church officers, and significant voices throughout the church and community. Many excellent Vision Statements have been destroyed (or worse, simply ignored) by governing boards that, because they were not involved in the process, did not accept the result.

You will certainly need to seek whatever official approval is appropriate within your church's system of governance. But beyond official approval, the planning committee should find a way to involve leaders in the explorations and feelings that have brought you to this point. Leaders and stakeholders need time to express their feelings, explore the options, and emotionally (as well as intellectually) endorse and support the proposed Vision Statement. Without such solidarity (united but not always unanimous), the planning committee should recycle the statement and seek to integrate the new views that have surfaced.

IMAGINING LIFE ACROSS THE JORDAN

God helped the Israelites imagine the Promised Land flowing with milk and honey, but the spies returned with reports of "giants in the land" (Deut. 2:20). There is always a tingle of uncertainty when congregations confront the unknown experience of a changing community. The "giants" are often more real in the fears of the congregation than in the actual situation in the community—but they are real enough to require effort in bringing them down to size. Even after you have named your Pillar of Fire and determined to move forward into the future, there are still challenges ahead as you try to see what it might be like to be in a new relationship with the community to which you feel called. Before your vision can take on concrete reality, there is more imagining to be done.

IMAGINATION EXERCISE 1: WHEN STRANGERS BECOME NEIGHBORS

Background and Rationale

Sometimes the strongest connections between seemingly disparate groups are located in foundational human experiences. People cross cultural barriers when they share the most basic human ventures—having children, bringing up families, struggling for employment, sharing sorrows, and celebrating successes. This is an exercise that countless congregations have enjoyed in innumerable settings. The task is simply to imagine conversations with neighbors about the most basic elements of life, beginning with something as mundane as the weather but exploring the deepest concerns as well. Crossing racial, cultural, and national boundaries begins with conversation between people who care about each other. This exercise invites you to explore and even experience those connections with the people who are part of your congregation and those who compose the community you have now identified as your own.

What to Do

With your Basic Timeline and your People Map before you, review what they tell you about community populations and trends. What are the possible connections between the people in the community and the people in your congregation through shared experiences, shared memberships, and shared activity?[10]

Explore as a committee the sorts of conversation you can imagine the people in your congregation having with the people in your community. Who among your congregation has ties to the community that might help your conversation? What would people from your congregation and people from the community say to each other about their strengths, about what they care about most, and about where each could understand and help the other?[11]

Remind yourselves of your experiences in interviewing members of the community and your congregation. Review what others said about their lives in the community. What have these observers told you about yourselves and your world that you might not otherwise have seen?

Act This Out. Ask two or three members of your planning committee to take on the roles of participants in a conversation between a community person and someone from the congregation. Imagine the conversation taking place in a neutral place, such as the laundromat or local school. Begin by talking about the bridges you have begun to identify in your common experiences, concerns, and memberships: children in school, job changes, traffic patterns, housing problems, and so on. Enact brief conversations—no more than five minutes. Pause after each imaginary conversation to discuss it. What concerns are participants raising? How are they raising them? Toward what end? Try another situation and discuss it. When you have finished, you can summarize the experience on the "Working Notes: Summarizing Possible Connections."

Reflection

When congregational members play at this make-believe conversation, it can be humorous and highly instructive, crossing generational and cultural differences with discovery of common concerns. With whom do you feel called to begin or expand your outreach? In what ways can you hear God's voice in the conversations you imagine between your congregation and the community?

Share Your Work

Make a storyboard that lists your brief dramatizations and notes what you learned about your connections with those who might become your neighbors. Ground your imagined connections in the actual community. Try out your insights on various persons in your congregation and with trusted persons in the community. Make this list a prayer list as you seek discernment for the direction of your ministry.

IMAGINATION EXERCISE 2: WHEN NEIGHBORS BECOME PARTNERS

Background and Rationale

Institutional partnerships can significantly expand congregational ministries. Partnerships are defined by the resources each partner brings to

WORKING NOTES:
Summarizing Possible Connections

Review your notes from Chapter Two, and create a list of the persons, groups, and organizations in your community with whom you wish to imagine future conversations. That list should inform your imaginative role-playing. After each enacted conversation, note what you learned.

Our enacted conversations (list your potential neighbors and what you talked about)	Points of connection (what draws us together)	Points of potential resistance (what keeps us apart)	Follow up (what to explore, with whom, and who will make the contact)

the relationship, but they are made possible by trust and understanding. Building strong coalitions is similar to developing conversations among good neighbors. We have worked in changing communities with congregations that discovered and cultivated partners of many sorts. Congregations have partnerships with almost every other imaginable community group—other congregations, social agencies, and local schools and colleges, but also government programs, volunteer efforts, local businesses, political leaders, banks and lending agencies, and many other local groups. You can never tell in advance who might become your "working friends" in developing ministry in the community to which you feel called.

This exercise invites you to imagine new institutional partners. In this process, you may imagine a bridge between the known past and the unknown future, and you may explore the essential ambiguity and risk in all relationships, but with a safety net. In previous exercises, you gathered a variety of information about your own resources and about local institutional needs. This information provides the basis for exploring your contributions to possible new ministries and for imagining the possible partners with whom you might work.

What to Do

Take some time to revisit your community maps and congregational timelines with an eye toward where the needs are, but also toward which aspects of community life in particular call out the passions of your congregation.

Ask yourselves questions about the work of other institutions that you might share. Which are the strongest and most viable, and which have the most in common with your goals? Also explore the marginalized and disadvantaged voices that might be strengthened by sharing with you. Then look back at what you learned about your building from the historical map and the timeline of your congregational space and ask yourselves questions about the resources you might offer:

- How have the uses of your building changed over the years?

- What space might be used in new or different ways to meet community needs?[12]

Go back to your analysis of your other resources as well, especially to see where you are doing very good work with surprisingly little money, perhaps because you have strong volunteer energy to harness and you have already found ways to work with community partners. Recall as well what seasoned observers suggested to you about your own resources and potential contributions. Look back at what others said about the community, about its needs and strengths, and about the role of your congregation. You can use the "Working Notes: Imagining Community Partners" to prepare your thoughts.

Act This Out. Explore potential relationships with several brief role-playing situations among members of your committee, and possibly with guests you invite. Select a potential institutional partner and an activity that might be undertaken together. Ask various members of your group to take on the roles of institutional leader, staff, client, financial supporter, political leader, pastor, church staff, volunteers, and others related to the institution and task you have chosen. Then set up an imaginary conversation in which the players discuss whether and how to undertake this new effort. There is one cardinal rule: no one should play her or his own role. Sometimes the stand-in catches the essence of the encounter and does it better than the real person, to the delight of participants. In several congregations with whom we have worked, the role-playing has been so convincing that the player has gotten a nickname from the performance.

The object of this role-play is to get imaginatively inside both your own concerns and those of your potential partners. Acting has the advantage of aligning you more closely with the thoughts and feelings of others. As you role-play the participants in community institutions, explore how they might feel about being partners with you. How does it help or hinder their goals?

WORKING NOTES:
Imagining Community Partners

Review what you learned in Chapters Two and Three about community needs, about your own resources, and about other institutions in the community. Use that to plan your role-playing.

Critical community need or passionate interest	Possible partner organization	Organization's key players	Their interests, concerns, and resources	Our key players	Our interests, concerns, and resources

Make a storyboard list of the situations you role play, and of other situations that were interesting to your group but you had no time to include. You should end up with a list of possible partners linked to the concerns and resources you might share. Note the issues and places where your community's needs and your congregation's assets come together. Where is energy already present that you can tap into or join? What did you discover about your current resources as limits and as possibilities? What new sources of support have been suggested by your conversations within and beyond the congregation? What are the possible partnerships that could be expanded or the partners who could be invited to join with you in ministry?

Reflection

Imagining partnerships should both expand your sense of what is possible and raise important questions. Your own vision should remain clearly in focus. As you think about life on the other side of the Jordan, consider who can most effectively help you do what needs to be done. Who can help you to find your new place in the community to which you have committed your future? The object is not simply to identify what is possible, but to explore the relationships that are consistent with your emerging vision.

Share Your Work

Post your storyboard list of interesting ministries and possible partners and invite response and discussion from members in the congregation and from others from the community who know you. Make your concerns and possible partners primary elements in your continuing conversations and prayers.

IMAGINATION EXERCISE 3: TESTING THE WATERS

Background and Rationale

Having acted out possible new connections with the community toward which you are journeying, you are now ready to imagine more concretely just what you might do with and in this community. You need the opportunity to think hard about where there is energy and passion for new engagement. Surrounded by the community maps and congregational timelines, the task of the committee in this exercise is to explore more fully the implications of the vision you have articulated. If this is the direction you have chosen, the vision you have for your future, what can you imagine doing that would bring that vision to life?

This is an upbeat exercise and a maximum number of congregational members and even friends from the community should be invited to participate. In this exercise, you seek to discover ideas, and more, to discern where there is energy and passion for new engagement. This exercise moves in two directions: the first phase expands your list of possible efforts, the second winnows that list of possibilities by capitalizing on the commitments of your members and friends.

What to Do

Begin by reviewing the imaginative conversations you had with members of your new community and potential partners. What issues have these conversations raised and what ideas have begun to emerge already?

Brainstorm Possibilities Allow a full meeting for a classic brainstorming session. You might suggest that each participant prepare by imagining a few "crazy ideas" and recording them on the "Working Notes: Seeding the Brainstorm." Encourage participants to suggest whatever new things they can imagine the congregation doing. Be sure to cover all areas of congregational life, such as youth and family programs, worship, religious education, fundraising, inviting new members, social outreach programs, public advocacy and service, fellowship groups, and the like. In classic brainstorming style, no dissenting comments are allowed. Pretend at least for the moment that anything is possible.

As each possibility is suggested, one or more participants should be its advocate, arguing strongly for it, even if they are not yet convinced it would work. This should be an energetic exercise, with vigorous, pointed, unrestrained, and playful imagination at work. Enjoy this moment when everything is imagined to be possible!

Focus the List   When everyone has been heard (in thirty minutes to an hour), phase two can begin. The leader or moderator of the meeting should call for a moratorium on new proposals and the group should explore the genuine commitments of the participants. Everyone should be asked to vote for the proposals to which they can imagine devoting time and energy, as well as for those to which they can see others in the congregation willing to commit resources and passion. Projects need not have majority support in the committee or the congregation as long as they can garner enough commitment to proceed. Conclude your deliberations by highlighting the changes and new initiatives that best catch the group's passions and that most clearly move toward embodying the vision you have identified.

Reflection

Think about which of these ideas seems most consistent with your congregation's values and history. Alternatively, which scenarios seem radically new but compelling? Which directions draw out the passions of

WORKING NOTES:
Seeding the Brainstorm

Brainstorming needs crazy, unexpected, even "irreverent" suggestions to stimulate imagination and break out of current logic. In preparation for the brainstorming event, take time to "imagine the unthinkable." For example, suppose the youth ran the whole church. Or suppose you had an endless supply of money for the next six months. Or suppose no one would object to changing the worship service.

"Crazy idea"	What changes would be necessary?	What might be lost?	What might be gained?

the congregation? How would you explain each scenario as a signal of God's leading?

Share Your Work

To arouse interest in this conversation, use every available means of communication—pastoral letter, sermons, announcements in worship, notices on bulletin boards, articles in congregational newsletters, notices on your church e-mail list, seasonal prayer materials, Bible study guides, even semaphore, if it helps. The committee needs to reach the congregation, to spark their attention, capture their imagination, and engage them in your conversation. You will need to test whether the priorities for action you have imagined can indeed find enough support to make them possible. In testing these possible priorities, your vision is already becoming a reality. Now it is time for the committee to proceed to the next exercise—a joyful celebration.

CODA FOR THE CONGREGATION: A TIME FOR CELEBRATION

Background and Rationale

The congregation that has stared down stark future options and adopted a new Vision Statement should be encouraged to celebrate its new beginnings. On the surface, nothing has really changed until the new ministry is launched. But if the Vision Statement has caught fire, then the congregation, like the children of Israel at the death of Moses, is prepared to give up something of the past in order to claim its new future. The members need a moment to celebrate their new identity, even before they fully understand its implications. Indeed, the congregation will need to "live into" its new Vision Statement over time—the subject of the last chapter.

What to Do

Lead the congregation in a significant worship experience (perhaps more than a single event) celebrating the commitments reflected in their Vision Statement. Sing hymns that tell of the future you see. Include testimonies and prayers and readings—whatever your own worship tradition might suggest. As the Israelites did in the final chapters of Deuteronomy, the congregation should look to its past successes, not as a nostalgic escape but as reassurance that the same God who walked with the people in past times will be their guide through the present and into a future yet unknown.

Reflection: Looking Ahead

Having opened your collective eyes to changes in the world in which you live, and having seen your own congregational life in new ways, you have begun to imagine how your ministry might become different. That is the essential commitment on a wilderness path toward change. That is the "promise" in "promised land." You are undoubtedly still feeling the surrounding wilderness, but along the way you have begun to discover the new resources you need and the new dreams that can sustain your journey. Rather than escape the uncertainties of cultural change, you have engaged them creatively. The long process of congregational adaptation still lies ahead. There are old ways to leave aside and mourn. There are new experiments to try and sometimes fail. There are new pilgrims and partners to welcome, and there are new stories to tell. Your transition is not done, but you are engaged, and you have enjoyed the journey!

Suggestions for Further Reading

1. Although the concept of institutional death and resurrection dates back to Good Friday and Easter, Mike Regele dramatically makes this view contemporary, in *Death of the Church* (Grand Rapids,

Mich.: Zondervan, 1995), with his strong attack on the patterns of repetition and resistance in congregations confronted by community change. His is a picture of death that comes by default rather than the sort of responsible death that includes good stewardship and appropriate mourning.

2. Gilbert G. Rendle, a congregational consultant with a foundation in organizational theory, provides a more extensive rationale for the wilderness experience in the process of change in *Leading Change in the Congregation: Spiritual and Organizational Tools for Leaders* (Bethesda, Md.: Alban Institute, 1998).

3. Ammerman, *Congregation and Community,* especially Chapter 8.

4. In advocating chaos as an essential element of congregational change, Gerald A. Arbuckle, S.M., provides several examples and models of congregations that have engaged their cultures for social change and have themselves been transformed in the process. See *Earthing the Gospel: An Inculturation Handbook* (New York: Orbis, 1990).

5. For more discussion of creative use of conflict in congregational life, see *Studying Congregations,* pp. 119–126.

6. In *Leadership Without Easy Answers* (Cambridge, Mass.: Harvard University Press, 1994), Ronald A. Heifetz argues that in institutions seeking to adapt to changing conditions, an essential leadership task is to create a "holding environment," where issues and options can be safely considered. See especially Chapter 5, pp. 101–124.

7. For additional help in defining the theological vision that shapes congregational life, see "Theology in the Congregation" in *Studying Congregations,* especially from p. 37 onward.

8. For a comprehensive overview of leadership disciplines that generate congregational renewal, see Jim Herrington, Mike Bonem, and James H. Furr, *Leading Congregational Change: A Practical Guide for the Transformational Journey* (San Francisco: Jossey-Bass, 2000). The authors provide an overview of various ways that communities find purpose and mobilize energy. A biblically and theologically grounded approach is provided in Danny E. Morris and

Charles Olsen, *Discerning God's Will Together: A Spiritual Practice for the Church* (Bethesda, Md.: Alban Institute, 1997).

9. For several alternative strategies that congregations can use to develop Vision Statements, see Jackson Carroll, "Leadership and the Study of the Congregation," in *Studying Congregations,* especially pp. 177–187.

10. For a more extended discussion of organizing cross-cultural mission in a postmodern context, see Darrell L. Guder, ed., *Missional Church: A Vision for the Sending of the Church in North America* (Grand Rapids, Mich.: Eerdmans, 1998).

11. For additional resources about sensitivity to community people, see *Studying Congregations,* pp. 63–66.

12. You can find additional help for expanding on the issues of sharing space in *Studying Congregations,* pp. 162–164.

CHAPTER FIVE

ACROSS THE JORDAN
Settling in the Promised Land

Entering the new land was not swift or easy for the people of Israel. In the biblical story, they endured the wilderness but still feared what awaited them on the other side of the Jordan. They had all the data from their spies' reports, and their leaders were full of the vision of a land "flowing with milk and honey." But the people were not yet ready to take the next step—crossing the river. They turned back until their leadership changed and their "members" found new commitments. The Jordan is not wide, but crossing takes effort. It took forty years before they were ready to get their feet wet and the rest of the biblical story to settle into the land.

This chapter is about settling into the promised land. At this point, many leaders concentrate on launching new programs of ministry, and we believe such fresh efforts are essential. Building on the interactive exercises of the previous chapter, we first offer a way of using your imagination to launch new ministries. Some congregations engage in this kind of anticipatory activity incompletely and almost by chance as they think about new programs. We want to highlight the practice and invite you to use it intentionally as an effective way to develop the habit of listening to many voices before making decisions that affect the speakers.

But we believe that as important as it is to undertake major program efforts, reshaping the congregational culture is equally important. The essential character of a congregation is not changed by rational analysis or leadership decision alone. New elements must be assimilated into the fabric and culture of everyday life, into the things you take for granted. In this final chapter, then, we invite you into new habits and practices of everyday ministry.[1] In the final analysis, congregations grow in transitional moments more because of who they are than because of the programs they offer. We suggest changes in four basic, rather mundane habits of congregational life—changes that will help you extend your hospitality far beyond the routine handshake at the door. Each practice points you to a kind of "table" you need to share with others—tables of food, tables that furnish the space you occupy, tables around which you debate and decide, and tables on which sacred bread is broken. On the surface, the practices we suggest may seem rather commonplace, but as they are absorbed into your routines, you will find that the vision you have developed is becoming reality. As you intentionally change habits, your feelings will follow, and these changes will result in congregations that embrace their changing community "naturally."

LAUNCHING A NEW MINISTRY: CROSSING THE JORDAN

Background and Rationale

Even after the people of Israel finally crossed the Jordan, they often suffered devastating defeats because they were not listening carefully for God's instruction. Every time you "cross over" into the promised land, you will need a calculated plan, but you will also need the spiritual conviction that God is the one calling you forward and that your congregation and community are ready to act. In this exercise, you can explore if and when you are ready to engage in a new or greatly expanded effort.

We suggest that, building on the brainstorming exercises in Chapter Four, you pick something from your list and playfully experiment with what it would be like to try that ministry. The experimental character of this exercise makes it flexible enough to be adapted to congregational decisions of many sorts. It invites members of the congregation to act out the prospects of a ministry and explore its implications even before you begin to implement it. The exercise includes four steps:

1. Focus on a particular area of ministry or possible new ministry.
2. Name the stakeholders—those individuals and groups that will be affected by this ministry.
3. Role-play a discussion in which the representatives of various stakeholders express their thoughts and feelings about the possible ministry.
4. Based on your evaluation of the experience, decide your next steps.

Congregations have used this exercise to consider a wide variety of choices, from the possibility of purchasing a new organ to responding to an invitation for civil disobedience. Once the practice is established, you may wish to revise and repeat it to explore and test the waters for additional programs and changes.

What to Do

This exercise should be entered as an imaginative experience, like children at play, to explore a possibility before you commit yourselves completely to a new undertaking.

Choose a Possible Project   The committee should select a potential activity—either something entirely new or an expansion of a present ministry—that gives concrete expression to the drafted Vision Statement. Because you have already done the Wilderness and Imagination Exercises, you have probably already generated a good list of possibilities. Choose an area that invites significant but not overwhelming congregational commitment. For this initial exercise, you might want to test a ministry that builds a bridge between the church and the newer residents in your changing community. You can subsequently return to exploring other alternatives on your list as well.

Your choice for a proposed ministry should make sense to your members, but at the same time it should stretch the congregation, pushing the limits of existing outreach into the new community. That is, based on what you know from your congregational timelines and community maps, this ministry could be your congregation's "next chapter." It should be consistent with your Vision Statement. It should be a ministry that is needed in the community and consistent with congregational faith commitments, in accordance with your investigation of populations and resources in your community and congregational profiles. On the basis of your previous interviews and conversations in the community and in the congregation, you should be able to name particular people who would be advocates for this ministry and whose views you could articulate. Again, avoid choosing something completely safe—dare to test the limits.

Name the Stakeholders   To whom would this project make a difference? Include on your list of stakeholders those people who would be partners in or assisted by the ministry, those who would be asked for supporting resources or endorsement, and those who would need to yield power to new partners. Because this is an exercise in sensitive listening, the committee should begin by identifying the voices that need to be heard. The following sorts of people appear on typical lists of stakeholders:

- Pastors and key board members (such as the treasurer)
- Clients or various people who might use this ministry
- Volunteers from the congregation or community who might assist
- Funders who might be approached to support the program
- Maintenance staff and others affected by the program
- Established members who always voice their opinions (such as the cranky committee chair, the dedicated idealist, and the like)

Stage a Role-Play   Create an imaginary meeting, a gathering of stake-holders, to discuss the proposed pilot project. The participants will take on stakeholder roles to argue for the positions they think would be taken by those key people. (The "Working Notes: Preparing to Role-Play a Stakeholders' Meeting" can be used to prepare.) This exercise needs to be staged (although sometimes an audience is not present) to encourage the players to take on the views of others and to speak from within the logic of the people they represent. Staging allows players to articulate feelings that might otherwise remain unspoken. In this process, both the participants and the audience can develop an appreciation for the views of others. This role-playing may be especially effective when participants take the roles of people with whom they strongly disagree.

Cautionary note: Enacting the views and feelings of other people can seriously backfire if the participants do not maintain a respectful stance toward the characters they are playing. This should be an exercise in empathy in which the players get close enough to the views of others that they can genuinely understand their differences more clearly. Because of the highly charged nature of this process, congregations often invite an experienced facilitator to guide this activity (which is how we have become involved), especially to assist committee members to enter and later to exit the event.

Unpack and Evaluate   In recording this event, note both the arguments and the feelings that are presented by the surrogate stakeholders. In subsequent discussion of the experience, identify the significant barriers that need to be resolved before the project is initiated. Some problems can be openly addressed: What resources are involved and where will they come from? What impact will the ministry have on existing programs and what might be lost in the trade? This exercise can serve as a window on the barriers that are difficult to express in ordinary public meetings and that could explode later and derail the project. Every community brings fears and prejudice into the uncharted experience of cultural change. If the participants have successfully played the thoughts and feelings of the stakeholders, you should have a solid foundation on

WORKING NOTES:
Preparing to Role-Play
a Stakeholders' Meeting

The pilot project we imagine:

Stakeholders who may have an interest in this project:

My role is to represent (name specific stakeholder):

My experience or source for information:

Arguments (pro and con) that this stakeholder would make:

Hopes and concerns that this stakeholder may have that might be hard
to express:

Biblical or faith resources this stakeholder might advance:

Allies this stakeholder might bring to developing this ministry:

For personal reflection only:
What emotional commitments do I bring to this exercise?

What results do I anticipate and hope for?

which to begin, and you should be forewarned of barriers and emotions that might later haunt your efforts. The story of Carmel United Methodist is a cautionary tale (see "Stakeholders and Decisions at Carmel").

Next Steps   Although this exercise may be used by the committee itself to explore both the passion and the problems in moving forward, by far its greatest impact comes when the role-playing is presented to a larger audience of leaders and members. In such a setting, particular people should be prepared to keep notes on newsprint, which can be used as a basis for discussion following the presentation. The audience-observers should be asked to record two sets of notes. The first set should relate to the emotional energy felt in the role-playing:

- Where is the positive energy? Which stakeholders have the vision and passion for this ministry? Is that vision and passion likely to catch fire among others?

- Where is the negative energy? Who is strongly emotionally opposed to this ministry? How widespread is that opposition?

The second set of notes should tap the substance of the discussion, attempting to summarize whatever consensus might emerge from the conversation.

- Describe the possible ministry as it emerged from the role-playing.

- What characteristics were suggested as the strengths and liabilities of this ministry per se?

- What are the lasting gains and losses for the congregation and for the community?

When you have completed your role-playing, you can summarize what you have experienced on the "Working Notes: Debriefing Your Gathering of Stakeholders."

STAKEHOLDERS AND DECISIONS AT CARMEL

Failing to imagine the responses of potential stakeholders can have unfortunate results. At Carmel United Methodist Church, new leaders attempted to move ahead with some key decisions without adequately consulting older members with strong commitments and long history in the church.

[Carmel Methodist's new pastor] saw that his congregation was beginning to be populated by a different kind of Carmel resident—more transient, but nevertheless highly skilled—and he wanted to move these newer people into congregational decision-making as expeditiously as possible. . . . From what we can tell, the actual election of new people to positions of authority in the congregation seems to have provoked little dissent. What provoked dissent was the elevation of those *positions* of authority over the *influence* of unofficial power brokers. . . .

The facilities planning fiasco revealed, however, that actual decision-making had moved out of those unofficial channels and into official committee structures. The planning committee had undertaken a careful process of consultation. People involved with all the programs of the church and people involved in every major committee were asked to offer their advice and desires. Whether this process intentionally excluded the older power brokers or whether they were inadvertently left "out of the loop," the result was the same. A major recommendation emerged without their advice and consent. They saw the process as "secretive" and under the manipulative control of the pastor. And compared to the relationship they had always enjoyed with pastors, their perception is understandable. Decisions were being made in committee meeting rooms at officially scheduled times, rather than in the informal conversations they had always enjoyed being privy to. A new arena of discussion had been created in the church, open to the many new skilled leaders in the congregation. The older leaders were not overtly excluded from this arena, but it was not their natural home. They managed to create enough dissension to prevent the adoption of the building plans, but they could not undo the transformation in authority structure that had taken place. [*Congregation and Community,* pp. 255–256]

WORKING NOTES:
Debriefing Your Gathering of Stakeholders

Where was the positive energy?		Where was the negative energy?	
Which stakeholders?	What do they bring to this potential ministry?	Which stakeholders?	What do they resist in this potential ministry?

Can you discern how God seems to be leading you?

What faith and feelings surround that choice for you?

Prepare a brief (one-line) prayer to share with your committee when you gather.

Notes about unpacking the experience: What are your personal feelings after participating in the role-playing exercise? Did you say all you wanted to? Were you fair with others? Were they fair with you? What do you need to say "out of role" to clear the air and complete the exercise?

Reflection

After all you have been through together, are you now ready to plunge into this new or expanded ministry that will reach new people in your community? If you will not implement this initiative, can you imagine another pilot ministry that is more likely to generate the necessary resources and commitment? This experience in discerning should be as much a spiritual as a rational decision. That is, do you see your new vision being embodied as you combine both practical planning and spiritual energy?

Share Your Work

Are you ready to launch this new ministry effort? If you have sufficient commitment from a few people who are willing to work, and general support from the congregation, then it is time to begin the concrete planning for launching the ministry. There will be many details to work out, resources to mobilize, people to consult, nuts and bolts to manage— planning for which you will need the help of many others in the congregation and the community. You may wish to deputize part of your committee to begin the organization of new bridge ministries between the old congregation and the new community. While the planning team may continue to take the lead in coordinating this work, it must now involve a wide cross-section of the congregation. As you move forward, remember that many of your best resources will be local and specific—such as denominational leaders, neighbor pastors, experienced managers, and good friends.

Beyond this programmatic work, however, what remains is the basic cultural work that will ultimately transform your congregation. It is these new practices and habits of ministry that will be the foundation on which your new life will be built.

NEW HABITS OF MINISTRY

When the people of Israel finally crossed the Jordan River, they had to learn to get along with their new neighbors. On that score, of course, theirs is a long, complicated, and at some points sordid story, and not a particularly good model for the rest of us. Thankfully, we are under no divine orders to get rid of the current inhabitants of our land!

Rather, we *are* under divine mandate to *love our neighbors.* Figuring out how best to do that is at the heart of what you have been doing on this journey. What remains, however, is the process of turning neighbor into kin, establishing the connections and forming the relationships, and altering old routines and moving the old furniture. If the exercises in the preceding chapters have led you to venture into new ministry, that almost inevitably means that new people and new ways of doing things will soon be "in here" rather than just "out there." Although you have crossed over into new land, you have not really left the wilderness behind. The exercises in this chapter are intended to assist you as you begin to welcome strangers into your midst—or as you learn to be strangers in this new land.

Many congregations that have successfully incorporated new members into culturally changing communities show remarkable similarities in their capacity to develop new habits of ministry. We have clustered their practices in four broad areas. These practices are like manners in behavior or grammar in language—the kinds of activities you practice until they are ingrained and assumed as normal. In our discussion of each of these practices, we explain what we learned from Nancy Ammerman's study of congregations in changing communities. We then offer a variety of specific ways to implement that finding. These methods are intended only to suggest the innumerable options you might develop. Look over our suggestions, activate your own imaginations, and select something that seems fairly easy. Start from your strengths and gradually add new practices that are more challenging.

For each set of new habits, we also offer a list of ways to measure your progress. These exercises are meant not to be ends in themselves (although many are inherently deeply satisfying) but rather to be means toward the kind of welcoming and hospitable congregation you have envisioned.

SHARING KITCHEN TABLES

What We Learned

We discovered in all the congregations examined in *Congregation and Community* that food and fellowship provide an avenue of acceptance into the religious community. Although the rituals of eating and the content of the food are often unique to each group, the act of sharing food is a symbolic incorporation and inclusion for everyone who participates. Both growing and declining congregations may enjoy gathering for food and fellowship, but in declining congregations, shared meals only reinforce existing ties and tend to exclude newcomers. Congregations that have adapted to changing cultures have discovered ways to open their tables.[2]

Adaptive congregations consciously and consistently include others in the fellowship of their tables. Transcending both social and theological differences, these congregations use the physical actions of preparing and eating meals—setting the table, sitting down, asking the blessing, distributing the meal, talking and playing, and even cleaning up—as inclusive ways to absorb newcomers into their lives. For adapting congregations, God is in the midst, not only above them but among them when they gather as a church family united in God's blessing for the common meal. In these congregations, the inclusive power of physical nourishment is not limited to meals (see "Sharing Kitchen Tables in Long Beach and Boston"). They show amazing creativity in the ways they provide food and drink in virtually every activity.

SHARING KITCHEN TABLES
IN LONG BEACH AND BOSTON

[At St. Matthew's Roman Catholic parish in Long Beach], the [Peace and Justice] Committee's most successful activity by far is their series of Monday night Soup Suppers during Advent and Lent. These evenings are significant not only for the money they raise, but also for the sense of community they foster in the parish. Many of the parish's gay members contribute their considerable cooking skill to the events, and here more than perhaps anywhere else . . . parishioners come together in an informal setting to share more of their lives than is possible on Sunday. . . . And here one can see the extent to which many social boundaries really do not matter; young and old, gay and straight, married and single—all enjoy these meals together. [*Congregation and Community*, p. 173]

[At Brighton Evangelical Congregational Church in Boston,] Sunday morning begins with breakfast, served to those who wish either the physical or social nourishment it provides. Both this meal and the van service that brings some parishioners to church are evidence of the congregation's care for its less well-off constituents. . . . The coffee hour held after each service is often a lively time of fellowship among all congregants. African American and Asian women hug and chat with elderly white women. A dozen or so young children of all races emerge from the nursery and proceed to wreak havoc playing games in and amongst the adults. After about forty-five minutes, congregants begin to trickle away. . . . BECC serves as a common meeting ground for people who return to very different homes and lives. [*Congregation and Community*, pp. 206, 202]

Through these physical symbols of sustaining life, adapting congregations learn the history, traditions, stories, and personal memories of others who are brought into their community. In the setting of the meal, they retell their memories of personal associations, stimulated by the warmth and symbolic power of the event. Food is a key to turn the lock of memory. Around the table, members of the congregation share their various journeys. And in the difficult, sometimes conflictual experiences of adaptation, members of the congregation return again to food and drink as a safe and sustaining place to quietly heal their differences and restore their common understandings and commitments to ministry together.

What You Can Do

- Be sure that food and drink are included in every possible congregational gathering, from the most elaborate dinner to the simple refreshments at a business meeting, from potluck dinners to receptions after church or after a funeral worship.

- Be intentional about exploring the diversity of cooking in the congregation. Bring recipes (or at least name tags) to your potluck. Create a congregational cookbook or a competition among the best cooks for their specialties. Celebrate the spices and special skills involved in producing particular dishes. Encourage culinary consciousness throughout the congregation.

- Celebrate holidays and historical moments with food and storytelling, mixing the goodies with memories around Christmas and Easter, for instance. Explore national holidays and the historical events of particular groups in the congregation and in the larger community.

- Get out of the ordinary. Take picnics, trips, and adventures into new places that are unfamiliar to everyone, new and old. Perhaps even plan costume parties on special days like Halloween or Mardi Gras, inviting everyone to don the safety of a mask, playing at being someone else and getting distance from their old selves. Include in these ventures moments of reflection over food and periods of rest.

- Make connections between worship and eating. Melt the worship in the sanctuary into your meals and social gatherings. Make explicit connections between liturgy and nourishment, and at the same time blur the margins of experience that separate the communion table and the common board.

Measures of Progress

At the simplest level, progress can be measured by the number and diversity of people who are eating together in various settings.

- In time, members of the congregation should begin to recognize and name each other's contributions, to know some of the history of other people's foods and some of the rituals of their family lives.

- The capacity to tell each other's stories is perhaps the greatest strength of an adapting congregation. When stories shared around the table begin to inform how people relate to one another and work together, food has begun to work its magic.

- The network of mutual understanding built in many conversations while breaking bread around the table and talking in hallways with a cup of refreshment is perhaps the most universal characteristic of congregations that successfully adapt to changing cultures.

SHARING TABLES, CHAIRS, AND SCHEDULES

What We Learned

For churches in changing communities, buildings can be a significant liability. With declining membership and lost revenue, church boards often delay maintenance on their physical structures far too long and the dilapidated character simply adds to the burden of the remaining membership. Further, many buildings were designed in a previous era, so they reflect the architectural tastes of a different culture and their space is allocated for the needs of programs of bygone times.

The greatest burden, however, can be the sacred memories that these buildings carry for many of the older participants. Even in a deteriorated condition, these buildings can be symbols of the congregation's golden era and, for many members, carriers of hallowed memories central to the members' lives—memories of weddings, funerals, baptisms, and more. Surrounded by such sacred space and burdened by deteriorating buildings that were poorly designed for contemporary programs, congregations in changing communities often find it difficult to imagine how their buildings might be changed to become places of warm welcome to new cultures and new participants. Recall the inventory and map you made of your space as you begin to imagine what could lie ahead.

At the same time, remember that new groups moving into a community are often looking for spaces in which to develop their own communal activities and that, in time, might shelter their own memories.[3] Programs that serve a neighborhood need space from which to do their work, groups that want to gather interested people for study or recreation or self-help need places to meet, and as congregations move forward, existing space can be used in new ways and altered to meet new program needs. When congregations find ways to open their doors— literally—their old buildings can give new residents a sense of continuity and acceptance. Some of the creative examples we have seen are recounted in "Buildings That Welcome Communities."

What You Can Do

- *Open your doors to community programs.* Seek out community groups that need space and can use your place to develop their programs. Work with them to find appropriate ways to share the cost of maintaining the building.

BUILDINGS THAT WELCOME COMMUNITIES

The doors of St. Matthew's, in Long Beach, are always open. And across town, First Congregational is a beehive of activity at nearly any time of any day. Brighton Evangelical Congregational's food and clothing ministries keep neighborhood people coming in and out of the building in a steady stream. And there are nearly always cars in Holman's parking lot. While the buildings of the declining congregations often hold precious memories for the members, the buildings of the adapting congregations symbolize their openness and their willingness to use their spaces for multiple purposes.

Inside, things have changed, as well. At Grace Baptist, the repaired and remodeled building symbolizes their fiscal health. At First Existentialist, a sculpted figure of a child joins numerous other pieces of art in the sanctuary. At St. Lawrence, the Advent stump, symbolizing the "root of Jesse," also symbolized the congregation's uprootedness and newness. And at First Congregational, the frequently used baptismal font came to symbolize the congregation's success in attracting "straight" young families, alongside their new gay and lesbian members.

At Good Shepherd Lutheran, in Oak Park, renovation of the building symbolized much of the progress—and the tension—of adapting to a changed community. In addition to making the building accessible, new classroom space was created in the basement to better handle the growing church school population. The tension emerged over what to do with the "founders' cross." Younger members had no particular attachment to it and were willing to see it disappear in the renovation of the altar area. Older members saw this attitude as a repudiation of them and of the church's past. In the end, the cross remained, more visible than ever, as a sign of an old identity cherished in the midst of rebirth. [Summarized from *Congregation and Community,* pp. 266, 273, 336]

- *Think about what specific new ministries you want to sponsor and what demands they will make on your space.* Your new interaction with the community might include child care, tutoring, meals, or art and music groups, and any of these will need useable space. Add ministries one at a time rather than trying to do it all at once.

- *Make the church visually appealing.* Adapting congregations attract people not by activities alone but by calling attention visually to what they are doing. Banners; advertising; bright, readable signs; night lighting; and distinctive paint on the trim all attract attention to the wide variety of activities that take place in the building.

- *Take pride in the building and expect others to take pride in being there.* From the flowers outside to the clean and attractive restrooms inside, make your building a place where others enjoy spending time. When you share your building with other groups, make sure you have a clear, mutual understanding of what the space means to each group and how it is to be cared for. The buildings of adapting churches can give participants a sense of self-respect and mutual appreciation.

- *Find ways to honor the memories that are embodied in your space.* Put old items to use in new ways or use the proceeds from their sale to carry on the purpose to which they were dedicated. Set up plaques or conduct mourning rituals when something important is going to disappear, or find a way to incorporate a symbol of the old item into the newly created space you are making.

Measures of Progress

- At the simplest level, progress can be measured by how your available space is maintained and used.

- More important, progress includes using that space in ways that are consistent with your vision. Whether activities are directly sponsored by the congregation or simply housed in its facilities, congregations engaged in intentional ministry see what happens in their buildings as vital to who they are.

- In addition, progress can be measured in the balance between available revenue for the support of the buildings and the uses to which you wish to put those buildings. When your own members, as well as others in the community, are willing to invest, you know you have found significant points of connection.

- Finally, progress can be measured in the way everyone involved talks about the building. When they walk around the property, the rooms and furnishings should remind them of stories, not only of days gone by but also of new ministries and newcomers.

SHARING BOARDROOM TABLES

What We Learned

Virtually every congregation studied in the Congregations in Changing Communities Project that significantly altered its identity and ministry also reorganized the way it made decisions and the people responsible for making those choices. For all congregations, this meant including new people, who represented different perspectives, into their decision-making groups. Inevitably, the inclusion of new people forced the established decision makers to change their commitments and expectations. Not surprisingly, every adaptive congregation experienced some level of internal conflict. A partial account is given in "Facing Conflict."

Let us be clear: internal conflict was one experience of every congregation that successfully adapted to changing circumstances. Conversely, all of the congregations that failed to adapt to external changes in the community reported internal peace, with no significant conflict. We are not suggesting that congregations must precipitate conflict in order to adapt. Rather, we are reflecting the reality that conflict comes with the territory.

FACING CONFLICT

In almost every instance, the congregations that have been newly born, reborn, or significantly changed have also had to work hard at creating and recreating their decision-making structures. The structural changes they have undertaken are often quite fundamental.

- Carmel United Methodist has dislodged an old elite. . . .
- Grace Baptist in Anderson has instituted strict fiscal policies. . . .
- First Existentialist engages in a rather constant round of retreats and debates. . . .
- First Congregational organized an elaborate educational and decision-making strategy. . . .
- City Baptist in Oak Park has created an intentional leadership training program. . . .
- Brighton Evangelical Congregational Church has reorganized its committee structure. . . .
- Hope Baptist in Atlanta is creating mission groups out of its old auxiliaries. . . .
- St. Lawrence parish in Gwinnett County has created a complex system of committees. . . .
- Northview Christian Life Church trusts much of its decision making to the pastor. . . .
- Good Shepherd Lutheran in Oak Park went through an extensive series of roundtables, forums, and educational activities. . . .
- Epworth United Methodist in Candler Park has been activating committees long dormant and inviting new people to participate. . . .

These congregations have recognized that lasting change will necessitate broad-based involvement by all the constituencies represented in the congregation. Where old structures protected old elites, new structures have been invented. And inventing new structures that dislodge old elites often leads to conflict.

Sometimes the conflict is prolonged and serious, leading to significant loss of membership. . . . Sometimes . . . conflict is simply assumed. It comes and goes, forming and re-forming around various issues, but not threatening the stability of the congregation in any significant way. . . . Other conflicts have been devastating and

> painful. . . . [Sometimes] painful church splits prepared the way for the decisions that would make change possible. . . . With troubling elements in the congregation gone, they could turn their energies to other, equally pressing matters. . . .
>
> This pattern of conflict stands in remarkable contrast to the peace and quiet of the non-adapting congregations. None of them has experienced any significant conflict in the recent memory of the congregation. . . . It is clear that attempting significant changes will involve conflict, and congregations unwilling to engage in that conflict will not change. [*Congregation and Community*, pp. 333–335]

Those that weathered the conflict best often placed high value on mutual education as a way of working together. In some cases, that happened because the backgrounds of the members (their formal education and professions) made them inclined toward planning, problem solving, and learning from differences of opinion. In other cases, it came through the intentional efforts of leaders to provide opportunities for members to learn together, to discuss their concerns, and to gain skills they needed to accept new responsibilities.[4] In all cases, a climate was created that encouraged people to state their differences and learn from experience. They learned how to use conflict constructively.

What You Can Do

- You can expand the number of groups with jobs to do and the number of participants who share in the decision-making process. Although this needs to be done in ways that are consistent with your denomination's rules of polity, inclusion of additional people brings new faces and voices into the conversation, which usually strengthens the legitimacy of decisions.

- You can create more situations where issues and concerns can be discussed informally. In some congregations, this means creating more organizational structures, such as task groups and committees. In other congregations it means expanding existing groups, such as Sunday school classes, prayer cells, fellowship groups, and the like. Adapting congregations simply generate more opportunities for more people to express their views more fully.

- You can plan congregational retreats to give people a chance to withdraw and gain perspective on the situation. Although some of these retreats may focus on organizational planning, it is also important to provide a variety of experiences that explore biblical texts, the mystery of God's presence, and the unknown character of working together in a new situation. Activities that place everyone on equally unfamiliar ground can be especially useful.

- You can ensure that every gathering includes time for food, fellowship, and spiritual reflection. Regardless of the purpose for which the group is organized, at least as much time should be given to building personal relationships as is given to working on tasks that confront the group. When the task is long past, the relationships will remain.

- As you approach significant new challenges, you can repeat the decision-making exercises presented at the beginning of this chapter. By acting out the voices of stakeholders, you allow feelings as well as arguments to be exposed and more fully understood by the rich diversity of participants sharing in the exercise.

Measures of Progress

- At the most basic level, progress is measured by the ability to make and implement decisions. But more than that, progress is seen when decisions are supported with financial and physical resources.

- Even when they disagree, members find ways to support the decisions of the congregation. Even if they provide no visible support, they are willing to keep the congregation's ministries in their prayers.

- The energy level remains high, people are able to laugh together, and participants enjoy the challenges of their common work.

- Aware of God's presence in mystery, participants come to appreciate more fully the diversity reflected in the group and the complexity in themselves.

SHARING SACRED TABLES

What We Learned

Worship remains the center of identity for most congregations, and worship often carries the most lasting imprint of the congregation's sense of itself and its history. For most newcomers to congregational life, worship is their entry experience. These people need to experience enough that is familiar that they feel at least partially included and sense that in time they could feel at home. At the same time, older members of transitional communities often report that changes in worship are the most painful experiences. Although intellectually they may wish to accommodate newcomers, if worship is radically and suddenly changed, they may feel emotionally and spiritually bereft.

All of the adapting congregations we studied experimented with different patterns of adjusting worship to incorporate new members without losing the old.[5] In some cases, the differences in worship styles and expectations were not great and most of the needed adaptation took place in programs and decision making. But even in those situations, bringing the experience of change into the worship life of the congregation was critical for sustaining enough spiritual energy for the work they were doing.

In other cases, the needed adaptation did involve important cultural differences in worship style. Where Anglo, black, and Hispanic cultures had distinctive forms, these were expressed and incorporated in the combined worship. To honor the unique heritage of each group, change often included a mix of diverse elements rather than an attempt to find any sort of middle ground. One church, rather than holding separate white and black worship services, as some consultants on multicultural ministry advised, found the Bible calling them toward inclusive worship. Each service now includes music familiar to both constituencies, and white members are learning a more relaxed sense of time. These changes in worship style have perhaps been hardest for older members to accept, but they seem to have created a sense of community that genuinely includes people of varying traditions.[6] The goal was not just to create something new, but to achieve a visible mixture of material from several sources, including healthy portions of what the congregation has "always done."

In other churches, old symbols have taken on new meaning. Baptisms at First Congregational in Long Beach, for instance, have become sacred moments for reflecting on the many kinds of families now included in the congregation.[7] Other churches have incorporated new breads into their celebration of communion, and still others have combined new and old elements in their worship space (recall the story of Good Shepherd in "Buildings That Welcome Communities," p. 163).

What You Can Do

- You can begin by understanding worship as more than a particular event performed by a few leaders. If worship is to express the passions and diversities of a changing congregation, it will have to begin with careful listening and planning, and everyone concerned will need to participate.

- You can return to your earlier study of how your worship traditions have changed over time. Choose an element that current members can remember having changed, and plan ways to change that element again to fit your new vision more fully. Move from small changes to larger ones.

- Always be ready to be surprised. Remember that God is both the audience and a coparticipant with you.

- Music is a particular challenge for blending worship experiences. Through music, you can celebrate the diversity of participation while moving toward experiences that are fresh for everyone. In negotiating new music, incorporate but don't be limited by the professional experience of the musicians with whom you work, the social unity of the choir, and the history and diversity of the existing congregational hymnody.

- Before, during, and after worship, you can explain new practices to the congregation, acknowledging the various historic streams of tradition that you are weaving into a single spiritual event. Such public explanations should help the worshipers claim the heritage of the past while showing how the various threads are woven into an even more challenging future.

- You can invent new symbols and traditions that embody your new experiences. Add a banner or other decoration, for instance.

- You can keep weekly worship events closely tied to everything else that is happening in the congregation. Sabbath worship is not where people gather for prayer but a gathering of praying people. By identifying the spiritual hungers that arise in all the places where members do their ministry, both individually and collectively, weekly worship can take on a natural vitality that includes the members' diverse journeys and traditions.

Measures of Progress

- Growth or decline in the number of participants provides one base index for progress. Who comes and why? How can more people be included?

- Emotional and spiritual investment in worship is equally significant but more difficult to measure. If worship is a drama, the worshipers are actors. Some participation may be clearly visible and audible, but other spiritual energy may be quieter and more reflective. Silence may indicate the deepest spiritual receptivity, or perhaps simple boredom.

- Listen for how music is heard and sung. The full expression of music begins before the worship and continues until the last participant has left the sanctuary. The most powerful music will continue singing in the hearts of participants long after the final "Amen."

- Representative feedback is critical. Often, people with extreme views—those who are most enthusiastic or most disturbed—are most likely to volunteer their opinions. Conversations with a wide variety of congregants can ensure that all views are represented. You should recognize, however, that talking about worship may take on the character of "explaining the joke." As in all your work, you should be selective in approaching respondents and sensitive in recording their views.

- Ultimately, you will know that worship is "working" as you see that nearly everyone finds something that sustains them in their ministry in the world.

CONCLUSION

Having engaged in the hard work of assessing the community in which your congregation ministers, and having turned a critical eye on your own resources and culture, you have dared to dream new dreams. Now you are daring to make those dreams reality by reshaping your everyday practices of faith. Sometimes strange words like *adaptation* can take on a mysterious and overwhelming quality, but what we hope you have experienced here is the concrete and ordinary routines of bringing new and old together in the work and worship of your congregation. In practices that stretch from the simplicity of breaking bread to profound worship in God's presence, welcoming new participants can create significantly fresh and powerful experiences. In processes as difficult as navigating conflict and redefining the use of space, every small issue resolved accumulates into broad and deeply shared commitments.

The story of the Israelites wandering through the wilderness is not the end of their biblical journey, but it is a memorable milestone near the beginning. People of faith are called to continue to listen for God's voice summoning them forward, challenging them to recognize new conditions, and rewarding them with fresh awareness of God's continuing presence. Along the way, you will need the habits of listening to your community, to one another, and to God that you have been developing in this effort. You will also need to continue the disciplines of sharing food, creatively using space, disagreeing constructively, and worshiping continuously. You will need to continue to dream new dreams and to seek the manna you need for the journey.

In the fall of 1999, as we completed our field testing of these exercises with congregations in San Francisco, our editor, Sarah Polster, spoke at a High Holidays service in her congregation. "This is the sort of relationship into which God is inviting us today," she said, "not one in which we are judged, but one in which we are released. Yom Kippur offers us the opportunity to let go of the attitudes and behaviors that create estrangements of all kinds—including estrangement from God—and enter into renewed contact and renewed possibility." We hope that this wilderness journey will provide the same experience for you.

Suggestions for Further Reading

1. Dorothy C. Bass has gathered together several essays that suggest the power of practices to shape the lives of individuals and institutions. See *Practicing Our Faith: A Way of Life for Searching People* (San Francisco: Jossey-Bass, 1997).

2. Intuitively, many congregations have understood the power of sharing their table through the practice of producing church cookbooks. While these publications produce income, they also provide comfort and bonding among contributors. Russell Chandler recognized the relationship of food to faith in his fresh reviews of congregations marked by the way they share their spiritual tables. See *Feeding the Flock: Restaurants and Churches You'd Stand in Line for* (Bethesda, Md.: Alban Institute, 1998).

3. In an Appalachian town exploited by outside forces, Mary Ann Hinsdale and her faith community have demonstrated how determined local leaders can use the meaning of place and space to reclaim their lives together, as she tells in *It Comes from the People: Community Development and Local Theology* (Philadelphia: Temple University Press, 1995). In *Urban Churches: Vital Signs* (Grand Rapids, Mich.: Eerdmans, 1999), Nile Harper reports on congregations across the country that have transformed their neighborhoods by creative use of existing buildings.

4. Charles Foster writes about this educational process in *We Are the Church Together* (Valley Forge, Pa.: Trinity Press International, 1996). He studied several multicultural congregations, giving careful attention to the ways diverse people learn from each other. Eric Wolf, in *The Bush Was Blazing but Not Consumed: Developing a Multicultural Community Through Dialogue and Liturgy* (St. Louis: Chalice, 1996), offers practical exercises to engage cross-cultural congregations and their communities in conceptualizing and resolving conflict, with unique sensitivity to various ethnic-racial differences.

5. In *Reinventing American Protestantism* (Berkeley: University of California Press, 1997), Donald Miller makes a strong argument that music and worship must always express the language and styles of the contemporary culture. His book is an exploration of the vitality he found in growing "new paradigm" churches, such as the Vineyard and Calvary Chapel. See also the more practice-oriented suggestions offered by Robert Webber in *Planning*

Blended Worship: The Creative Mixture of Old and New (Nashville: Abingdon Press, 1998). In addition, Thomas G. Long shows how several of the practices we suggest come together within worship. See *Beyond the Worship Wars: Building Vital and Faithful Worship* (Bethesda, Md.: Alban Institute, 2001).

6. See *Congregation and Community,* pp. 215–218, for more of this church's story.

7. First Congregational Long Beach is described in *Congregation and Community,* pp. 174–185.

THE AUTHORS

CARL S. DUDLEY served as a pastor in Buffalo and St. Louis and on the faculty at McCormick Theological Seminary in Chicago before joining the teaching and research faculty of the Hartford Institute for Religion Research, Hartford Seminary. As a consultant and author, he has written on small churches, community outreach ministries, church growth, biblical themes, and congregational studies, and he draws heavily on his book *Basic Steps Toward Community Ministry* for this publication.

NANCY T. AMMERMAN joined the Hartford Institute for Religion Research, at Hartford Seminary, in 1995, after teaching for eleven years at Emory University's Candler School of Theology. Her early writing looked at the world of conservative religious movements, but for much of the 1990s she concentrated on understanding the dynamics of congregational life. Her 1997 book *Congregation and Community* provides the springboard for this present volume.

INDEX

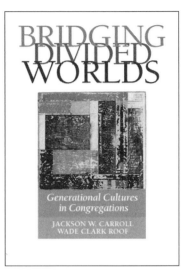

Bridging Divided Worlds
Generational Cultures in Congregations
Jackson W. Carroll
Wade Clark Roof

$23.95 Hardcover
ISBN: 0787949906

"I'm delighted to see this collaborative book by two of the nation's most distinguished scholars of religion. Through a cleverly designed combination of personal interviews, case studies, and survey data, Carroll and Roof show us the huge impact of generational differences on the ministries of local churches. This fine book should be 'must reading' for clergy, religious leaders, and students of religion."

—ROBERT WUTHNOW, Princeton University, and author, *After Heaven: Spirituality in America Since the 1950s*

"By looking closely at significant historical events, sociological data, and anecdote, the authors help us understand how we have come to the present generational diversity that is affecting our congregations today. This very readable, pastorally sensitive study is a needed addition to the growing body of literature that is attempting to make sense out of present day religious life in the United States."

—REV. ROBERT J. SILVA, president, National Federation of Priests' Councils

One of the hottest and most confusing issues in spiritual communities today is the tension between generations, who bring with them different understandings of faith, different levels of religious literacy, and different expectations of what a church or synagogue should be and do in the lives of its members. In some cases, these tensions are dividing congregations into separate institutions that share little other than the church roof over their heads. In this book, Wade Clark Roof, the leading author on issues of generation and faith, and Jackson Carroll, one of the most respected voices on congregational leadership and dynamics, will share the learnings from their comprehensive study into generational dynamics in congregations and show how some congregations are finding ways to bridge the different worlds the generations inhabit.

JACKSON W. CARROLL is a professor at Duke University Divinity School, where he teaches congregational studies and sociology of religion.

WADE CLARK ROOF is professor of the sociology of religion and chair of the prestigious Religious Studies Program at UC Santa Barbara.

[Price subject to change]

OTHER BOOKS OF INTEREST

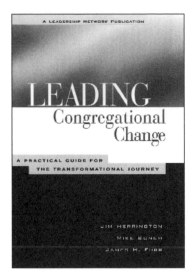

Leading Congregational Change
A Practical Guide for the
Transformational Journey
Jim Herrington, Mike Bonem,
James H. Furr

$23.95 Hardcover
ISBN: 0787947652

"Leading a church to change from being tradition- or program-driven to being purpose-driven is a task filled with all kinds of potentially explosive and divisive issues. This is a book you ought to read before you change anything."

— RICK WARREN, author,
The Purpose-Driven Church

When two-thirds of this nation's congregations are witnessing flat or declining membership rates, something has to change. But bound by tradition we often resist the very change our congregations need to thrive. Our challenge: revitalize our congregations and create a new center, one that will give church leaders a solid foundation for growing and reinvigorating congregations in the joyful spirit of Christianity. Written by three distinguished church consultants, *Leading Congregational Change* offers proven processes and tools for accomplishing this goal and revitalizing churches of any size and across the broad spectrum of denominations.

With this much-needed handbook, the authors brilliantly combine their experience guiding dozens of churches through the change process with both the study of Christian disciplines and the sophisticated understanding of such important business thinkers as John Kotter on leading change and Peter Senge on learning organizations. In this eminently readable book the authors have distilled their insights and practices into simple but powerful concepts for leading congregations, whether long established or recently formed, through profound change.

JIM HERRINGTON is executive director of Mission Houston, an interdenominational, multicultural pastoral effort to transform the city of Houston.

MIKE BONEM is president and cofounder of Kingdom Transformation Partners, a church consulting and training firm based in Houston.

JAMES H. FURR is senior church consultant with Union Baptist Association and adjunct professor of sociology at Houston Baptist University.

[Price subject to change]

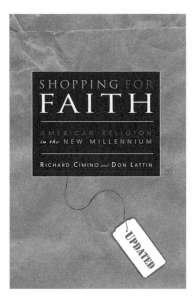

Shopping for Faith
American Religion in the New Millennium
Richard Cimino
Don Lattin

$15.95 Paper
ISBN: 0787961043

"*Shopping for Faith* is as good as it gets in assessing the U.S. religion scene at millennium's end. Cimino and Lattin present a picture of multiple trends headed in often contradictory directions."

> —ROBERT ELLWOOD, emeritus professor of religion, University of Southern California

"Cimino and Lattin are well positioned to give us a broad sounding of the contemporary spiritual scene in America. Once we have seen, via this book, the many different waters of the river of living spirit

- we appreciate the richness of all the ways through which God renews the currents of faith
- we see how often we have been immersed in the eddies—our particular practices
- we look further downstream, across the millennium, and see our differences meld into one ocean."

> —RAM DASS, author and spiritual teacher

The United States is one of the most religious countries in the world and has been for a long time. What has changed is the environment in which we hold and practice our faith.

American religion flourishes in a consumer culture, and presents us with a bewildering array of choices as we navigate the shopping mall of faith. The authors identify dozens of trends that will shape American religion in the next century and bring together the latest research and intimate portraits of Americans describing their beliefs, their religious heritage, and their spiritual search. With warmth and style the authors document how consumerism shapes religious practice—from conservative evangelical worship to the most esoteric New Age workshop.

RICHARD CIMINO is editor and publisher of the much-quoted newsletter, *Religion Watch* (www.religionwatch.com), which researches trends in contemporary religion. He has worked extensively as a researcher and freelance writer for various publications, including *Christian Century* and *Religion News Service.* He is the author of *Against the Stream: The Adoption of Christian Faiths by Young Adults.*

DON LATTIN is the award-winning religion writer for the San Francisco *Chronicle.* Over the past twenty years he has interviewed thousands of Americans about their religious heritage and spiritual search. He was a fellow at the program in Religious Studies for Journalists at the University of North Carolina at Chapel Hill and has also taught religion reporting at the Graduate School of Journalism at the University of California at Berkeley.

[Price subject to change]